IN
EMERGENCY,
BREAK
GLASS

ALSO BY NATE ANDERSON

The Internet Police: How Crime Went Online, and the Cops Followed

IN

EMERGENCY,

BREAK

GLASS

What Nietzsche Can Teach Us
About Joyful Living in
a Tech-Saturated World

Nate Anderson

W. W. NORTON & COMPANY
Independent Publishers Since 1923

For information about permission to reproduce selections from this book,
write to Permissions, W. W. Norton & Company, Inc.,
500 Fifth Avenue, New York, NY 10110

For information about special discounts for bulk purchases, please contact
W. W. Norton Special Sales at specialsales@wwnorton.com or 800-233-4830

Manufacturing by Lake Book Manfacturing
Book design by Chris Welch
Production manager: Anna Oler

Library of Congress Cataloging-in-Publication Data

Names: Anderson, Nate, author.
Title: In emergency, break glass : what Nietzsche can teach us about joyful living in
    a tech-saturated world / Nate Anderson.
Description: First edition. | New York : W. W. Norton & Company, [2022] |
    Includes bibliographical references and index.
Identifiers: LCCN 2021051576 | ISBN 9781324004790 (hardcover) |
    ISBN 9781324004806 (epub)
Subjects: LCSH: Nietzsche, Friedrich Wilhelm, 1844–1900. | Life. | Happiness. |
    Joy. | Technology.
Classification: LCC B3317 .A5175 2022 | DDC 193—dc23/eng/20211116
LC record available at https://lccn.loc.gov/2021051576

W. W. Norton & Company, Inc., 500 Fifth Avenue, New York, N.Y. 10110
www.wwnorton.com

W. W. Norton & Company Ltd., 15 Carlisle Street, London W1D 3BS

1 2 3 4 5 6 7 8 9 0

For Gordon

CONTENTS

IN
EMERGENCY,
BREAK
GLASS

One

BURN THE BOATS

The Tiger's Eye

MY LIFE SHRANK SLOWLY—UNTIL ONE DAY IT BECAME too small.

I used to feel that, in stitching me together, the Universe had rather gone out of its way. To know that my atomic makeup was forged in the furnaces of the primal starfield and that my childhood geography was shaped by glaciers dragging themselves north through Wisconsin for centuries—well, it all suggested a lot of effort. I felt a duty to make that work count, to change history for the better, to "bestride the narrow world like a Colossus"—or, at least, to do more than watch epic amounts of television.

Under the influence of the 1980s band Survivor, I adopted the Eye of the Tiger. I *would* change the world—and I'd enjoy doing it. Yet one day I woke to find that *carpe diem!* had been replaced by "How many emails can I answer before noon?"

It happened so gradually. When at last I noticed, I looked around with a shock to find that my life had taken on a certain indoor quality—comfortable but quiet and air-conditioned.

Perhaps it was just a case of "becoming a realist with a mortgage," but it felt more deflating.

Technology did not cause this lifestyle contraction, but it served as means and enabler. I was the product of a revolution—in communication, media, and practically everything else—that had driven us all indoors during the past century. Even in a "friendly" midwestern town of immaculate houses, I didn't meet my neighbor for 3 years. Our encounter required another intervention of the Universe: a freak blizzard that drew us all outside to clear several feet of snow from our driveways. My neighbor had until then existed for me as a head inside a Lexus, but he now burst forth in triumph from his garage astride the largest yellow snowblower I have ever seen. The winter's disruption sparked some dormant sense of community, and my neighbor offered to clear my drive. But we spoke only for a moment; the snarl of the machine prevented further connection. I went back inside, pleased with the help but wondering if life might not be better had I shoveled alongside my neighbor, in amiable conversation, for an hour.

The Internet allowed me to write from home, and I made a fair living as a technology journalist whose commute could be as short as sitting up in bed to crack open the laptop. There was peace and freedom in this, and there was limitation. It required effort to make new friends; it required effort simply to escape the house. After a decade working from home, my days were spent before computers, my nights spent before televisions, and my free moments spent itching to unlock a tablet or mobile phone.

My grandparents had farmed the fertile fields of Iowa, slaughtered hogs, and sold Ethan Allen furniture. They lived into their nineties without ever watching more than *Wheel of Fortune* and the evening news. They had little need for screens, yet my life had become screens. Without them, I could no longer read the paper, write a letter, play a game, talk to friends, work a job, check the weather, make a to-do list, read a novel, listen to music, watch a movie, or take a photograph. The world's tactile richness was reduced to polished pieces of glass.

Atoms, galaxies—the Universe is ever restless. Yet there I was, day after comfortable day, sitting still. I sat on couches, beds, and chairs. Some days I mixed things up by moving from the couch in the basement to the couch in the living room or from the chair at my desk to the chair in my bedroom. I became a champion seat-sitter, a connoisseur of the sedentary, the kind of person with strong opinions about lumbar support and chair height. The gap between the raw activity of my grandparents' life and my own tap-click existence had become a canyon.

While doing all that sitting, I lost the ability to say "no" to words. Each day I moved my eye across tens of thousands of them—hundreds of emails, dozens of news articles, several long-form magazine pieces, a continuous stream of text chat from my colleagues. I was living what, as long ago as 2009, researchers at the University of California–San Diego had described: "Americans consumed information for about 1.3 trillion hours, an average of almost 12 hours per day," which corresponded to "100,500 words and 34 gigabytes for an average person on an average day." This seemed unbelievable, but not by much.

An alarming number of my dinner comments began with the phrase, "I was just reading an article about that . . ." As a former graduate student in English Lit, I felt terrible about this because my growing information inhalation coincided with an inability to get through books. Yet I had always loved books. My shelves buckled beneath the weight of P.G. Wodehouse, Graham Swift, and W.G. Sebald, yet much of the material I spent my time reading each day was two steps above a Buzzfeed "Which Hogwarts house are you?" quiz. Words had become a fire hose, blasting me constantly in the face. They were exhilarating but exhausting; when you need a drink, a single glass of clean water offers more refreshment.

At the end of a day spent among those 100,500 words, I felt incapable of sustained focus. My screens then offered their own remedy: an unending stream of video content. This came with costs, including an even stronger sense of information overload. In the bad old days, the live TV schedule had simply washed over me; I felt no responsibility for it. Now, watching a show was a matter of choice, and the completist in me had to watch every episode. I began to dread multi-season shows. "Too much of a commitment!" I thought. As soon as one show was complete, ten others jostled to take its place.

Still, sustained watching was easier than sustained reading, and I feasted like a vegetarian in a tofu factory. I streamed every episode of *Lost* and spent the next year telling my wife that anyone who wrote for the final three seasons should be banned from Hollywood. I binged on complete runs of *Friends*, *Frasier*, and *30 Rock* (twice). I even watched Gordon Ramsay shout his way through four seasons of the "reality" show *Hell's Kitchen*, an act for which I am still doing penance.

I wallowed in more material than I could work through in a dozen lifetimes: 40-hour video games, board-gaming podcasts, and Bob Dylan albums; iPad apps to try, Kindle books to read, and Epicurious recipes to bake; British murder-mystery TV shows, interactive *New York Times* explainers, audiobook versions of *The Odyssey* narrated by Ian McKellen. The new technologies of abundance stood ready to engage my attention anytime, anywhere, on any device.

But my attention, the searchlight of consciousness, also came under assault by new technologies of interruption: text messages, group chats, Slack messages, emails, and app notifications. It reached a point where I could go only minutes without something on my computer or mobile phone beeping, buzzing, or intruding itself. And I didn't turn any of this off, because it felt good to be given this succession of tiny gifts, each one a surprise. In a world where people checked their phones 80 times a day—or every 12 waking minutes, on average—the simple act of focus became countercultural.

Looked at in one way, I was living the dream: My life demanded little physical exertion, it required no risks, and it piped endless information and amusement right to my eyeballs. It was, in that favorite word of Silicon Valley CEOs, "frictionless."

But seen from another angle, I had tap-clicked my way into a lifestyle of comfort, abundance, and immobility—and found it intolerable. Perhaps you have felt the same discomfort, looking up from yet another spam email to wonder: What has become of the wonder and danger of life? What has become, in other words, of our collective Eye of the Tiger?

An Unexpected German

Back in college, I had read—or, to be strictly accurate, *passed my eyes across the pages of*—a fair bit of German philosophy. I found it . . . not quite to my taste. Reading it taught me three things:

1. If you're going to doze off during lectures about Feuerbach, don't sit in the front row.
2. Schopenhauer is a *huge bummer*.

3. Plowing through both Kant and Hegel in the same week is like being raked across the face by barbed wire.

These negative experiences, which were goosed by additional reading in (shudder) Heidegger and (twitch) Adorno, gave me solid justification for avoiding someone like Friedrich Nietzsche. My life had enough problems without German philosophy, which was often stupefying even when its authors *hadn't* gone insane.

Yet Nietzsche's books had such delicious names—and his pithy quotes showed up in such a surprising number of Etsy craft shops— that I couldn't quite dismiss him. Kant wrote the impenetrable *Critique of Pure Reason*, while Hegel penned the impenetrable *Phenomenology of Mind*—but Nietzsche wrote books with cheerfully reassuring titles like *The Gay Science* and *Daybreak*. And Nietzsche was the kind of bomb-thrower who could write "I am no man, I am dynamite!"—and mean it.

So during one of those aspirational moments when I put down the laptop and picked up a book, intent on Improving My Mind, I cracked open Nietzsche's late work *Twilight of the Idols*. It seemed a promising place to begin.

For one thing, it was written in the last months of Nietzsche's sane life, and it functions as a sort of "greatest-hits" record of his philosophy. As everyone who ever listened to 1980s hair metal knows, you *desperately want to avoid most bands' full albums*, which are stuffed with filler. On the other hand, the greatest-hits record collects all those power ballads you actually want to hear. Given Nietzsche's prodigious mustache and wavy locks, I figured that what was true of hair metal might also apply to nineteenth-century German philosophy.

Second, *Twilight of the Idols* is short. Do not undersell the power of brevity. For instance, when he was a young man, my father once shanked a tee shot so badly that it passed through a stand of pine trees and hit another golfer on the posterior just as the unfortunate fellow bent over to line up a putt. My Uncle Jack, who related this story with gusto at every family gathering I ever attended, eventually whittled it down to a single look— pop-eyed with a pursed mouth and arched eyebrows—that stood in for the surprised golfer at the moment of impact. This look could be deployed without narrating a single word of the broader tale, and the family would reliably dissolve in laughter.

Third, *Twilight of the Idols* bears the undeniably terrific subtitle *How to Philosophize with a Hammer*. Dispel any vision of smashing away with sledgehammers, however; the image is of a mallet tapped like a tuning fork against the great idols of our culture. Will they ring out with a clear, sweet note or with "that famous hollow sound which speaks of inflated bowels"? Nietzsche's hammer sounds the common wisdom of the human herd and finds it wanting—especially the pervasive idea that "the good life" is "the easy life."

So I dove in and read, on the very first page, "If we possess our *why* of life we can put up with any *how*. Man does *not* strive after happiness; only the Englishman does that."

Utilitarians such as British philosopher John Stuart Mill were Nietzsche's target. Nietzsche objected to Mill's ethical emphasis on providing the greatest good to the greatest number, which seemed to him like an argument for making the most possible people "happy." But Nietzsche's own recipe for happiness lay in not having to *be* "happy" all the time. Ease, comfort, pleasure— they are all fine as far as they go, but they are certainly not life's *point*; creative exertion, even struggle, makes life matter. Every revolutionary, from Jesus to Che, can tell you that.

This did not sound insane. Indeed, it was terrific stuff, and what's more—Nietzsche could *write*. (He is often listed as one of the greatest German prose stylists after Luther and Goethe. Indeed, he says this of himself.) From across a gap 130 years wide, Nietzsche called out to me.

I raced through *Twilight of the Idols*. Next up was *On the Genealogy of Morals*, a three-essay set that was provocative in the best way, and *The Anti-Christ*, which was provocative in the worst. Then came *Ecce Homo*, the autobiography finished weeks before madness clouded Nietzsche's mind; it features chapter titles like "Why I Write Such Great Books" And "Why I Am So Clever." Next came the Gospels-meet-self-help mashup *Thus Spoke Zarathustra*, which was exciting enough that the German government issued an edition to soldiers during World War I. Then came *The Birth of Tragedy*, a piece of fascinating philosophical propaganda favoring some very specific Greek tragedians while blaming Socrates for sending Western culture off the rails. I plowed through the aphoristic works *Beyond Good and Evil, Daybreak, The Gay Science*, and *Human, All Too Human*. (Do not read them, as I did, straight through.) Finally, I dove into the *Untimely Meditations*, in which the young Nietzsche argued passionately that knowledge was not a good in itself; it was only good if it *helped us live*. This was relevant, as my browser history reminded me that I had spent half an hour that morning clicking through articles on myxomatosis. I have never owned a rabbit.

I stopped haranguing my wife about the failures of the *Lost* writers' room, and I started haranguing her about Things Nietzsche Had to Say On Whatever Topic You Just Mentioned. She endured it with long-suffering generosity.

I had plenty of material for these uninvited harangues because Nietzsche made pithy comments about everything, including

God (dead), morality (immoral), and his own abilities (amazing). He had thoughts on the early Wagner (sublime), the later Wagner (a chump), enemies (valuable), suicide (freedom), and sitting still (the real sin against the Holy Spirit). He loved evolution but hated Darwin; he hated Christianity but put up with Jesus.

And he had the most fascinating, terrible life.

Nietzsche was born in the town of Röcken, Prussia, in 1844. His father, Carl Ludwig, was a Lutheran pastor who died 5 years later at the age of 36. His death was due to an unspecified "brain" issue; Nietzsche would always wonder if madness or illness ran in the family line.

Young Friedrich was raised in a household of women that included his sister, Elisabeth, his mother, a grandmother, and a pair of aunts. When he gained a scholarship to the famous boarding school Schulpforta in 1858, he moved away from home for most of the year and embarked on an old-fashioned educational program that was infamous for its rigor. As a 14-year-old, Nietzsche began his Schulpforta lessons daily at 6:00 a.m. and was encouraged to speak to the other boys in Latin and Greek.

Nietzsche's own health, even as a teenager, was never good. His name is listed 20 times in the Schulpforta illness log between 1859 and 1864, and Nietzsche required a week on average to recover from each episode. Treatments at the time, despite the school's international reputation for excellence, remained as retrograde as some of the teaching methods. "At Pforta they were treating Nietzsche's ghastly episodes of chronic illness, his blinding headaches, suppurating ears, 'stomach catarrh,' vomiting, and nausea with humiliating remedies," writes biographer Sue Prideaux. "He was put to bed in a darkened room with leeches fastened to his earlobes to suck blood from his head. Sometimes they were also applied to his neck." Nietzsche suffered through.

Though the school doctor suggested that blindness lay ahead, Nietzsche wore dark glasses to protect his aching eyes and continued his studies.

Schulpforta was not a "fun" place for a child to learn, especially one not into the culture of sports, hikes, and patriotism, but it did give Nietzsche a solid educational grounding in Hebrew, Greek, Latin, theology, and German literature. He took his degree and went off to university at Bonn, where he drank beer with a proto-fraternity called Franconia, gained a small dueling scar on the bridge of his nose, and lost his Christian faith. Nietzsche's discipline was philology, which at the time was a mix of history, literature, and languages, and he wrote long papers on obscure Greek topics. When an influential professor of his left Bonn for Leipzig, Nietzsche realized what a waste his sabre duels and beer drinking in Bonn had been, and he headed for Leipzig, too, to get serious about philology.

This proved a wise choice. Nietzsche so excelled at his work that his professor recommended him in 1869 for the open chair of philology at the university in Basel, Switzerland—and Basel made Nietzsche an offer. Nietzsche was just 24, the youngest man ever to be offered a teaching post at the school. He hadn't even earned his degree yet. With a prestigious job offer already in hand, however, Leipzig granted Nietzsche his doctorate in March 1869 and shipped him off to Switzerland.

Despite his own bouts of ill health, Nietzsche took a leave of absence to serve as a medical orderly in the 1870 Franco-Prussian War, where he promptly contracted typhoid and diphtheria. He was obviously a genius, but he could never bring himself to write as a professor "should," and his 1872 oddity *The Birth of Tragedy* was not the first book expected of a promising scholar. It was an embarrassment to the scholastic guild, and few students signed up for Nietzsche's seminars after it appeared. His migraines, vomiting, eye pain, and insomnia grew so bad that he relied on friends and family to read to him and to take his dictation; he missed long periods of class and walked around Basel with tinted spectacles and a green eyeshade. He began to feel that philology was sapping his strength—he had been pushed too early into the herd of "scholarly oxen."

Out of this crisis came *Human, All Too Human* in 1878. It was a highly readable work, dense with gnomic aphorisms that forced readers to think through issues along with Nietzsche rather than lapping up spoon-fed conclusions. The book explored the ways in which all-too-human needs and experiences lay behind most transcendental ideals. It had nothing to do with Nietzsche's nominal discipline of philology; his colleagues wondered what the young professor thought he was doing.

One of the ideals Nietzsche came to loathe was ease. He saw politicians of his day promising a comfortable life to everyone. But at what cost?

> If the enduring homeland of this good life, the perfect state, were really achieved, it would destroy the earth from which a man of great intellect, or any powerful individual, grows: I mean great energy. When this state is achieved, mankind would have become too feeble to produce genius any longer. Should we not therefore wish that life retain its violent character, and that wild strengths and energies be called forth over and over again?

Nietzsche's shadow side emerges here—his characteristic redemption of violent impulses and savage energy as the motive force behind full-fledged human excellence. The ways in which he puts these views can veer quickly from "provocative" to "unsettling." It is also clear that he was no democrat. His inter- est was less in the mass, the commoner, the *herd* than it was in the individual, the genius, the *exception*. We will have to peer more carefully into these attitudes later, but the point is clear enough: The good life is not the enervating comfort of respect- ability and ease.

Nietzsche himself gave up such a life the next year. In 1879, under the pressure of illness and despair, he resigned his chair in Basel and became an intellectual vagabond on a modest pension. He sold most of his things. Hauling his few trunks of belong- ings between the homes of friends and the more affordable sort of European guesthouse, Nietzsche never worked a "job" again. Instead, he sought places where he might feel well, scribbling thoughts into notebooks during long walks in the Alps and along the Italian coast. Aphorisms suited him, because he could work on them between attacks that might leave him retching and help- less for days. Doctors continued to warn Nietzsche that blindness was a likely result of his tremendous eye pain; they counseled him to stop reading and writing. He could limit his reading, but writing had a hold on him that no doctor could break.

Nietzsche published *Daybreak* in 1881, refining his mastery of the aphorism as he wondered what kind of humans might be produced by a lifetime of comfort. "Are we not," he asks in the book, "with this tremendous objective of obliterating all the sharp edges of life, well on the way to turning mankind into *sand*? Sand! Small, soft, round, unending sand!"

Looking at his contemporaries, Nietzsche saw an almost reli- gious obsession with ease. Comfort had become an undisputed good, even for many German Christians. In 1882, a year in which he pursued a one-sided romance that proved both farcical and devastating, Nietzsche published *The Gay Science* and again preached against this attitude:

> If you experience suffering and displeasure as evil, hateful, worthy of annihilation, and as a defect of existence, then it is clear that besides your religion of pity you also harbor another religion in your heart that is perhaps the mother of the religion of pity: the religion of comfortableness. How little you know of human happiness, you comfortable and benevolent people!

There wasn't much comfortableness for Nietzsche. His health continued poorly, almost no one read his books, he had no job, and his sister, Elisabeth—whom he playfully called "Llama"—got engaged to an Aryan supremacist named Bernhard Förster. Nietzsche hated bigots, and so he hated Förster; when Elisabeth married him in 1885, Nietzsche did not attend the wedding. The newlyweds moved to Paraguay, where they oversaw an explicitly racist colony called Nueva Germania. Nietzsche cut off contact.

He still wrote furiously, putting out a major project a year despite his ever-shifting maladies, but his vaunted productivity came to look increasingly like mania. In late 1888, when Nietzsche claimed to feel a surge of good health and high spirits, he wrote not one work but four, each increasingly visceral and erratic. Weeks after finishing his self-justifying autobiography *Ecce Homo*, which argues that he was one of the greatest human beings to ever live, Nietzsche mailed a set of extremely odd Christmas letters. Many of them stressed that he was about to become the most famous person on Earth.

On January 3, 1889, just 44 years old, he collapsed in the winter sunshine of a Turin piazza. (The story—perhaps apocryphal—goes that he saw a local cabman whipping a horse, and Nietzsche threw himself in front of the whip and then fell to the ground.) After he was taken back to his rented rooms, Nietzsche was never truly lucid again. A friend from his Basel days came down to Italy and took Nietzsche home by train. Nietzsche spent the following 11 years in obvious mental agony, both in a Jena asylum and at his home. His sister returned from Paraguay and eventually gained control over both her brother's body and his works. Elisabeth created the Nietzsche Archive to raise her brother's stature, and she published a Nietzsche biography with obvious inaccuracies. She collected and controlled access to his letters, then published *The Will to Power* from material left in Nietzsche's notebooks. She began to host literary salons in the family home even while her brother groaned and roared upstairs. During this long period of insanity, Nietzsche became famous; his books sold across Europe and money poured in. He knew nothing of it.

Nietzsche finally died in August 1900. Elisabeth, who continued to distort his legacy for decades, survived until 1935, helping to turn Nietzsche's thought into a kind of proto-Nazi ideology of domination. Adolf Hitler attended her funeral.

Nietzsche's life was often sad, sometimes grotesque, but his undeniable talent was forging genius from his own pain.

As an academic prodigy, Nietzsche looked set at 24 for a comfortable life in a comfortable town, well paid and well respected, his schedule regulated like a Swiss clock. Over the coming decades, he planned to tunnel through an avalanche of words, excavating a scholarly path forward with help from the library and the bookshop. His labor would be mental and verbal, largely sedentary, the interiority broken only by weekend train trips into the country to visit Richard Wagner or to climb a local peak.

But thanks to both temperament and biology, Nietzsche turned his back on these plans. His personality found little joy in the academic world he had proved so gifted at inhabiting, while his subterranean illness burst forth so often that the "religion of comfortableness" was not a live option. If life's true joys could only be found in hedonism and control, then Nietzsche was doomed, for he could experience neither.

As a professor, Nietzsche felt crushed beneath the weight of information overload. He thought endlessly about his relation to what we might today call "content." He sought freedom—and his own voice—through an embrace of rereading, restriction, and forgetting.

Nietzsche broke free of his job and reputation when he left Basel after a decade, but he also broke free of the regimented interiority of so much knowledge work. He engaged the world with his body and not just with his rational mind, learning to think in powerful new ways that relied on movement, emotion, and desire. Despite ill health, Nietzsche wrote more passionately about joy than has any other philosopher I have ever read. In all three of these ways, Nietzsche felt sharply and surprisingly relevant to me, and his diagnoses of his own problems sometimes seemed like diagnoses of my own.

The Second-to-Last Man

In 1883, Nietzsche made his most extended pitch against the easy life, and he did it in the form of a parable.

Thus Spoke Zarathustra has become Nietzsche's most famous book. In it, the ancient prophet Zarathustra descends from his mountain cave. (Zarathustra is simply another name for Zoroaster, the Persian sage behind the ancient Zoroastrian religion.) In language heavy with biblical allusions, he attempts to interest the local villagers in his philosophy. It . . . does not go well.

It is time for humanity to set itself a new goal, Zarathustra tells the befuddled villagers.

> The time has come for man to plant the seed of his highest hope. His soil is still rich enough. But one day this soil will be poor and domesticated, and no tall tree will be able to grow in it. Alas, the time is coming when man will no longer shoot the arrow of his longing beyond man, and the string of his bow will have forgotten how to whir! I say unto you: one must still have chaos in oneself to be able to give birth to a dancing star. I say unto you: you still have chaos in yourselves!

Zarathustra wants to call forth this productive chaos. Only through motion and power and risk can one find the energy to become something new.

Now, Nietzsche has a reputation as a negative thinker; he's counted as one of the great "Masters of Suspicion" along with Marx and Freud. Everything that a culture takes as obvious—that religion is good, for instance, or that pity is noble—Nietzsche wants to interrogate. His answers are often the inverse of society's valuation, which is why he calls his project the "Revaluation of All Values."

But Nietzsche's ultimate goal is positive. It involves saying a great Yes to life even in the absence of transcendent meaning or purpose. He preaches—and "preaching" is certainly the word for much of this—the best possible version of humanity. This new kind of human is referred to as the *übermensch*, a word variously translated as "overman" or "beyond-man" or (unfortunately, once Clark Kent appeared) "superman." It is this *übermensch* that Zarathustra preaches to the village.

But this is not the inevitable future of individual and collective humanity. Nietzsche thinks it equally likely that humans will retreat from the difficult path forward and take refuge in the "most contemptible" form of being, which he calls the "last man." This way of life values safety, ease, health—values that can come at the cost of striving, risking, and creating. It is the sort of life in which even one's vices are mundane. Grand passions have been extinguished—one cannot even *fight* well anymore!—and people indulge their weaknesses rather than discipline them. The result is a search for something contemptible: comfortable contentment.

"Nietzsche regards the failure to draw a distinction between happiness and contentment as especially disastrous," writes Nietzsche scholar Michael Tanner. "For him, the only happiness worth having is that which is the by-product of strenuous efforts in various directions, efforts undertaken without a thought for the happiness they might produce."

Zarathustra therefore warns the villagers:

> The earth has become small, and on it hops the last man, who makes everything small. His race is as ineradicable as the flea-beetle; the last man lives longest. "We have invented happiness," say the last men, and they blink . . .
> One still works, for work is a form of entertainment. But one is careful lest the entertainment be too harrow-

ing. One no longer becomes poor or rich: both require too much exertion . . .

One is clever and knows everything that has ever happened: so there is no end of derision. One still quarrels, but one is soon reconciled—else it might spoil the digestion. One has one's little pleasure for the day and one's little pleasure for the night: but one has a regard for health.

One of the curiosities of Zarathustra's argument is that the "last man" is not a race of cosseted weaklings that will simply die out. No, the lifestyle of the "last man" *works*. Its emphasis on safety, society, health, and ease produces a class of beings that, like beetles, are almost ineradicable. But who wants to be a beetle?

The crowd does.

"Give us this last man, O Zarathustra," the villagers shout back at him. "Turn us into these last men!"

They are not wrong to want such things. To those who have labored without ease or security or those who have lived in isolation or with illness, the goods of the "last men" are worth pursuing. But I think Nietzsche is right to suggest that perhaps these goods are only way stations on the human journey, not the terminus.

As I read this passage, I recognized that my life and longings had indeed become cramped, degenerating into a quest for mere "happiness." I worked but did not strive; I read but only became clever; I regarded my health to the point of neuroticism. Had I become, staring at my screens day and night, one of those who heard about higher and harder things and simply "blinked"? Was I like the villagers, who heard Zarathustra's "despicable" description of the last man—and loved it?

If not yet the "last man," then I was something close. Call me the "second-to-last man."

Too Much to Know

We live, as the poet W.H. Auden noted years ago, in *The Age of Anxiety*. One recent symptom: the profusion of weighted blankets—an Amazon search brings 3,000 results—that offer relaxation beneath their comforting constriction.

Imagine yourself in bed beneath an especially heavy version of one such blanket. You wish to rise up to *carpe* the *diem*, but you can't even raise an arm. The blanket does not weigh enough to smother, but it cannot be kicked free, shaken loose, or shuffled out of. It traps you, comfortably immobile, in the softest possible prison.

For many of us, this is how "information overload" feels. It is a kind of smothering—not a spur to action but an inhibition of it. Conditioned by science, the Enlightenment, and a commonsense idea that "knowing what you're doing" is better than "*not* knowing what you're doing," many modern cultures fetishize information. Does anyone today feel dumber than when they make a mistake for which *they could have just Googled the answer?*

Any attempt to get up off the couch of the "last man" and take risky action in the world must confront the challenge of information, which today threatens to overwhelm, distract, and derail us. "Information has become a form of garbage," writes the communications professor and critic Neil Postman in his 1992 book, *Technopoly*, "not only incapable of answering the most fundamental human questions but barely useful in providing coherent direction to the solution of even mundane problems."

Technology made this possible. It gave us the scroll and its linen, the codex and its vellum, the press and its paper, the smartphone and its screen. With each innovation, the past piled up around us. Consider the sheer volume of the information that fills our mental rooms: Text messages. Podcasts. Snapchat. Netflix. Facebook. Instant messages. Emails. New books—hundreds of thousands a year. Old books—Google has digitized the contents of entire university libraries. Fifty million albums of streaming music. Every magazine article ever published. The 6 million articles (just in English!) on Wikipedia. YouTube. The *New York Times*—and its massive archive. Every other major world newspaper. The entire World Wide Web. And so little of it is necessary to live. Without some criteria for using, sifting, and shaping it, our information-rich past and present may simply press on us until we live like hoarders, surrounded by detritus but treating it like treasure.

Even ancient authors complained about too many books and not enough time. But the issue became acute during the Renaissance. As Harvard historian Ann Blair notes in her book *Too Much to Know,* "The discovery of new worlds, the recovery of ancient texts, and the proliferation of printed books" made Renaissance knowledge into something truly overwhelming.

Perhaps it's no surprise, then, that thinkers such as René "Cogito Ergo Sum" Descartes tried to burn the past down, building up a philosophy using only the universal human experience of conscious thought. Why spend years laboring through Latin declensions, the Greek alphabet, or the Hebrew *hiphil* when you could ground everything in "I think, therefore I am"? No books, no tongues, no God—not yet, anyway. Just a man, thinking his way through a winter night in 1619.

Descartes's own frustration with attempts to wring the world's information from its store of books is palpable. "Even if all knowledge could be found in books," he wrote, "where it is mixed in with so many useless things and confusingly heaped in such large volumes, it would take longer to read those books than we have to live in this life and more effort to select the useful things than to find them oneself." And this even though Descartes didn't have TikTok videos to distract him.

Things only got worse after Descartes's day, and Nietzsche felt the acute burden of too much information. He saw clearly how one's life could be spent exploring the most distant tributaries of knowledge. As a philologist, he knew that mastering the ancient Greeks was a lifetime task—to say nothing of everything written since.

After a decade spent teaching the youth of Basel, both at the university and at the local *Pädagogium*, Nietzsche was fed up. What mind could *think* under the pressure of everything that one "should" read, see, or hear?

"The sum of sensations, knowledge, and experiences, the whole burden of culture, therefore, has become so great that an overstraining of nerves and powers of thought is a common danger," he complains in *Human, All Too Human*, a book that he said was dictated with his head bandaged and in pain. "A diminution of that tension of feeling, of that oppressive burden of culture, is needful, which, even though it might be bought at a heavy sacrifice, would at least give us room for the great hope of a new Renaissance."

Reflecting on this period in his later autobiography, Nietzsche saw himself in thrall to a cramped and useless approach to knowledge. He and his fellow "scholarly oxen" spent their lives like ruminants who grazed only on books, but to no life-giving purpose. After a decade of this work, what had been mastered? Fragments of ancient drama and philosophy that gave few answers to Nietzsche's own questions—or to his own suffering.

"Ten years behind me during which the nourishment of my spirit had quite literally been at a stop, during which I had learned nothing useful, during which I had forgotten inordinately much over a trash of dusty scholarship," Nietzsche complained.

> Creeping meticulously and with bad eyesight through antique metrists—that is what I had come to!—I was moved to compassion when I saw myself quite thin, quite wasted away: realities were altogether lacking in my knowledge, and the "idealities" were worth damn all!

What Nietzsche came to see, in the futility of his quest to master knowledge, was that modern people need (as we might put it today) a practical theory of information management. This is not a luxury for eggheads; it is an important component of a goal-directed life. Nietzsche tackled the issue in his early essay "On the Uses and Disadvantages of History for Life." One feels the personal anguish radiating through his introduction, where Nietzsche wonders if too much time given to study might not cripple one's life. He senses this intuitively, but he fears being ungrateful to truly impressive gains in knowledge collection and transmission since the Renaissance; after all, one does not want knowledge and culture *destroyed*. Yet he cannot shake his "tormenting feelings" that overstuffing one's life with information might be "injurious to it, a defect and a deficiency."

Nietzsche concludes that "instruction without invigoration" and "knowledge not attended by action" is a luxurious waste. It must be "hated by us." The point of life—even a scholarly life— is not to get through content; it is not to master material. It is to learn how to live. And then *to actually live.*

Looking around at philology, Nietzsche concluded that much of our study of the past was frivolous. "We need history, certainly," he wrote, but:

> We want to serve history only to the extent that history serves life: for it is possible to value the study of history to such a degree that life becomes stunted and degenerate—a phenomenon we are now forced to acknowledge, painful though this may be, in the face of certain striking symptoms of our age.

Such "striking symptoms" of information disorder are easy to spot in our own age. Ask anyone who plops into an armchair after dinner, phone in hand, hoping to vegetate for 10 minutes—but who looks up to find an hour has passed. As a one-off event, this may simply be "human, all too human" of us; as a regular occurrence, it looks pathological. If, as Annie Dillard once wrote, the way we spend our days is the way we spend our lives, then many of us are spending our lives consuming content of fairly dubious long-term value.

For me, it was streaming video. Not because I was watching an unusual amount of it—compared to most Americans, at least, I watched moderate amounts—but because it became both an uncomfortable comfort and a beautiful burden. It became so easy to watch "one more episode" that I often awoke with a start at 3:00 a.m., finding that I had fallen asleep on the couch during one too many episodes of *Breaking Bad*. Stumbling upstairs with foul breath and a foggy mind, I did not feel liberated by technology. Yet when the next night came, I did it again.

Watching TV in the bad old days, when you had to take whatever was on and put up with advertising breaks, had at least this virtue: It could wash past you. It was, by its nature, fleeting. But streaming TV meant the cavalcade of comforting, ad-free images never quite came to an end. The next episode awaited; a new "must watch" show always beckoned. The more I watched, the further away the end of my queue looked. I felt active anxiety about adding shows that ran for more than three seasons to my watchlist; who could handle 150 more episodes of *anything*?

Was this abundant life—or was it "stunted and degenerate"?

Trying to "keep up" with culture has always been hard; in the Information Age, it is a delusion. In the end, our best attempts to master information make us mere tourists in the kingdom of knowledge. In *The Gay Science*, Nietzsche reckoned with his own desire to keep up with information. He faced the truth that this is already impossible. In fact, keeping up grows *increasingly impossible* with every new piece of knowledge or culture.

"Perhaps we philosophers, all of us, are badly placed at present with regard to knowledge," he writes. "Science is growing; the most learned of us are on the point of discovering that we know too little. But it would be worse still if it were otherwise—if we knew too much; our duty is and remains, first of all, not to get into confusion about ourselves."

That's the heart of the approach that Nietzsche develops toward knowledge: Know yourself. Know your limits and embrace them. Reject the burden of any information that does not contribute to *living* your life. That means setting aside huge swaths of content. Nietzsche's theory of information management emphasizes slow reading, rereading, *not* reading—even *forgetting*. To truly live, we must be willing *not to know* many things.

Separating the information that gives life from the information that kills became Nietzsche's obsession in the years after his eyes failed him and he stepped back from the academic life. His eye pain and migraines eventually "put an end to all bookwormishness," he wrote later. "For years I ceased from reading, and this was the greatest boon I ever conferred upon myself!"

For those schooled in societies that value education to an almost pathological degree, this can be difficult. It was difficult for Nietzsche, too, whose identity had been so tied to his scholarship. But in his enforced info-cocoon, and the physical pain that accompanied it, Nietzsche found his mind at work on new problems that *meant* something to him. He found, in a word, himself.

"That nethermost self, which was, as it were, entombed, and which had grown dumb because it had been forced to listen perpetually to other selves (for that is what reading means!), slowly awakened; at first it was shy and doubtful, but at last it spoke again," he later recalled. "Never have I rejoiced more over my condition than during the sickest and most painful moments of my life."

In the section labeled "On Scholars" in *Thus Spoke Zarathustra*, Nietzsche reflects on the academic identity he left behind in Basel.

> I moved out of the house of the scholars, and I even slammed the door behind me. Too long did my soul sit hungry at their table; I am not, as they are, trained to pursue understanding as a kind of nut-cracking. . . . I am too hot and burned by my own thoughts: often it almost

takes my breath away . . . but they sit coolly in the cool
shade: they want in all things to be mere spectators and
are wary of sitting where the sun burns down upon the
steps. Like those who stand in the street and gape at the
people passing by, they too wait and gape at thoughts that
others have had.

This is Nietzsche in a nutshell: the call to stop sitting in the
shade, to stop being a spectator to one's own life, to *think*, to
speak, to *live*. It rang true to my own experience, as I had left a
graduate program in literature some years before for the same
reasons. My experience began in the joy of great books, but it
ended among seminars on the daily doings and religious politics of the Long Parliament during the English Civil War of the
1640s. I was pursuing knowledge as if it were nutcracking, dig-
ging out the nutmeats to form a tiny hoard of high-protein eso-
terica. Out of it I could cobble together papers on Renaissance
history, theology, or politics—occasionally even on literature.
Professors argued whether any of this should even *have* a point
or whether we studied the past simply for its own sake. My soul
sat hungry; after 4 years, I too left their house with the door
banging behind me.

The position is not anti-intellectual. Even in the years of
his solitary wanderings around Europe on a minimal pension,
Nietzsche lugged a massive trunk that he called the "clubfoot"—
filled entirely with those books he could not bear to be without.
But his approach is intensely realistic about the frailties of our
"human, all too human" minds and life spans. It puts information in its proper place, *serving life* rather than becoming an end
in itself.

Sit as Little as Possible

Imagine an English evening in the late 1700s. On his journey home from boarding school, the young William Wordsworth pinches a rowboat. It is tied to a willow tree on the shore of Ullswater in the Lake District. The summer holidays have arrived, night has draped itself upon the landscape, and the stars reflect in the water. The future poet finds himself powerfully tempted; he slips the boat's halter from the willow and eases out into the lake for a joyride.

He muffles the creak of the oarlocks until far from shore, then strokes hard enough that his tiny craft goes "heaving through the water like a swan." A craggy hill blocks out everything beyond, but as Wordsworth rows past this pedestrian piece of land, a cliff face towers into view behind. Suddenly, savagely, it blots out the moon. Wordsworth, alone in the dark in a stolen boat, feels a thrill of existential dread—until his phone vibrates against the wood floor of the boat.

Bzzt bzzt.

It's a text message from Wordsworth's classmate, Ted Sanderson, who like Wordsworth is trekking home from Hawkshead School for the summer. Wordsworth, on the brink of a mystical experience, ignores the message.

He recenters himself on the boat bench. He releases the oars. He looks up at the sheer cliff face that has been revealed, as though by Providence, to measure out the small size of a human life. He feels the uncaring geologic power brooding in the stone. He is Having A Moment.

Bzzt bzzt.

Messages arrive in bunches, lighting up the phone screen. Each new one draws his eye, no matter how he fights the impulse. Wordsworth looks back at the cliff, then sighs and unlocks the phone.

"Haha! Cropper fell off his pine," says the first text. "Into a puzzle!"

Who Cropper is, why he was on a pine, and how he fell into a puzzle are not explained.

"Damn autocorrect," says the second text. "Off his pony. Into a puddle. A PUDDLE!!!!"

Ted has attached a selfie of his pink-cheeked face beside that of the unfortunate Cropper, who appears to be the servant carting him home. Cropper is, as the messages have promised, soaking wet in the mud.

Wordsworth smiles despite himself. He feels the night chill seep through his shirt as he glances back at the cliff. It looks less sublime now, no longer a rocky demon one might storehouse in the mind for years.

Wordsworth paddles frantically back to shore and runs homeward through the meadows without any "grave and serious thoughts." He suffers nothing from "huge and mighty forms that do not live" but which "like living men moved slowly through my mind / By day, and were the trouble of my dreams." Wordsworth's solitary experience upon Ullswater is never immortalized in poetry as

> a huge cliff,
> As if with voluntary power instinct,
> Upreared its head. I struck and struck again,
> And, growing still in stature, the huge cliff
> Rose up between me and the stars, and still

With measured motion, like a living thing
Strode after me.

Some of our most precious and most delicate mental states can only exist without interruption. Sublimity, religious ecstasy, varieties of cosmic dread, wonder, rapture, even our sexuality: These are altered by the presence of the buzzing smartphone. Can we listen to Gabriel Fauré's Requiem in D Minor *in the same way* while receiving a series of texts? Can we see our child's fourth-grade chorus concert *in the same way* when watching it through a screen as we record? Can we hike up Mount Katahdin *in the same way* while constantly capturing the moment in pictures?

We live different lives when our experience of the world is mediated or interrupted. Unfortunately, for all the good they do, our digital technologies are expertly crafted attention grabbers.

Nietzsche was exceptionally sensitive to the need for uninterrupted immersion in our physical existence, and he found suspect anything that removed us too completely from this immersion. Even reason, he came to argue, was tied to our physicality. We are not, and should not try to be, "brains in a vat." We need to *own* our embodiment.

"We do not belong to those who have ideas only among books, when stimulated by books," Nietzsche writes in *The Gay Science*.

It is our habit to think outdoors—walking, leaping, climbing, dancing, preferably on lonely mountains or near the sea where even the trails become thoughtful. Our first questions about the value of a book, of a human being, or a musical composition are: can they walk? Even more, can they dance? We read rarely, but not worse on that account. How quickly we guess how someone has come by his ideas; whether it was while sitting in front of his inkwell, with a pinched belly, his head bowed low over the paper—in which case we are quickly finished with his book.

Whenever his health allowed, Nietzsche took long summer walks in the mountains around Sils Maria, Switzerland, or long winter walks along the sea in Genoa, Italy. He thought as he walked; he took notes that became his books; he conceived his most uniquely Nietzschean doctrines at specific physical locations. You can still visit the rock on the north side of Lake Silvaplana where Nietzsche discovered the idea of "eternal recurrence."

"*Sit* as little as possible," he wrote weeks before his collapse into insanity. "Give no credence to any thought that was not born outdoors while one moved about freely—in which the muscles are not celebrating a feast, too. . . . The sedentary life— as I have said once before—is the real *sin* against the holy spirit."

Simply moving around—challenging enough in these screen-first times—is not enough, however. Nietzsche worries that humans have become such creatures of reason and self-reflection that they are incapable of committing their full attention to the present moment—of *inhabiting* experience rather than reflecting upon it.

Switching off this reason-heavy self-consciousness is a key concern of his first book, *The Birth of Tragedy*. It nominally concerns the development of ancient Greek tragedy, but it's about as far from an "academic" book as San Francisco is from Boston. It opens with a description of two forces that Nietzsche names after the Greek gods Apollo and Dionysus. Apollo, the deity of sunshine and sculpture, is associated with order, control, and reason, "that restraining boundary, that freedom from wilder impulses, that sagacious calm of the sculptor god." Modern humans have developed too much of the Apollonian temperament, however; they risk cutting themselves off from one another and from nature by a heightened and controlled self-consciousness that can never release itself from its own tension.

Dionysus, in contrast, is associated with wine, emotion, chaos—and a loss of the self-consciousness that divides us from nature and from each other. "Not only is the bond between man and man sealed by the Dionysiac magic," Nietzsche writes. "Alienated, hostile, or subjugated nature, too, celebrates her reconciliation with her lost son, man."

One doesn't want a purely Dionysian experience of life, which would amount to the dissolution of the self, a lack of control over one's mind and body, and the loss of reason's gifts. But Nietzsche argues that an overly Apollinated humanity needs *more* of the Dionysian. "These poor creatures have no idea how blighted and ghostly this 'sanity' of theirs sounds when the glowing life of Dionysiac revelers thunders past them," he writes.

Nietzsche himself was no Dionysian reveler. His poor health meant no alcohol; his isolation meant few parties. Certainly there were no drunken torchlight processions to sacred groves. So far as we can tell, he had sex only a handful of times. But he found in music a release so powerful that he repeatedly championed the power of art to save us from ourselves. While listening to the best of Wagner, he could set down the burden of being himself; he could embrace the ecstatic unity of creation championed by the old religions of Greece and Rome.

This explains Nietzsche's crank-ish hatred of Socrates. In the world of philosophy, this is a bit like harboring a secret spite toward cupcakes. And yet Nietzsche loathed Socrates. It was the ancient Athenian philosopher who had, Nietzsche said, pushed Apollonian reason to the forefront of philosophy, where it has stayed ever since. Socrates was a "typical decadent" who set "'rationality' *against* instinct," Nietzsche writes. "'Rationality' at any price as a dangerous force that undermines life."

Which is to say, simply: Logic cannot give us Wordsworth's sublime terror in a rowboat. Reason itself becomes self-interruption of and internal commentary upon our own sense experience. Reality becomes too *thought about to be felt.* There is wisdom in the body that the mind knows nothing of.

Nietzsche calls us to combine the Apollonian and Dionysian tendencies, to restore a balance between controlled rationality and a more ecstatic physical immersion. Does this ring true to us today as we tap our hammers against the idols of our culture, sounding out the false notes?

Many of our most common technologies, designed as they are to capture attention, make sense immersion a challenge. We are complicit in our own captivity. Texts, emails, and social media posts constantly interrupt us because we have allowed them to—and we cannot resist attending when they do so.

Our most popular information technologies exert a subtle, persistent pressure on our psyches to *look away from the world* before us. Our minds may be pushed forward, anticipating that next text, email, or tweet. They may be pulled elsewhere, staring at Instagram posts from our friends' apparently more beguiling lives. Or they may simply be distracted by games, sounds, and videos. What information technology does *not* usually encourage is a relaxed openness to the physically local, the here, the now.

Our screens are now so compelling that we are looking at them *while looking at other screens.* Nielsen data from 2019 revealed that 88 percent of people surveyed said they used a "second digital device" while watching television. Our screens present us worlds more stimulating and more novel than our own; they have become our tutors in *elsewhere-ness*.

The "elsewheres" on offer through the Internet can be tremendous gifts. Yet our local reality, even in its tedium and awkwardness, remains the place that matters most for human connection. As MIT researcher Sherry Turkle found in her research into technology use and community, "The ties we form through the Internet are not, in the end, the ties that bind. But they are the ties that preoccupy." It is worth considering whether our devices do too much to pull us away from the physical spaces we inhabit.

Nietzsche hated all "elsewheres." He referred to them as "other worlds," whether offered by Plato (the Forms), Jesus (heaven), or Kant (the thing-in-itself). Anything that offers itself as something more real than the world of appearances we perceive through our senses distracts us from the here, the now, the embodied, *the truly real*. Elsewheres invariably disguise from us the fact that we are creatures of the earth. Much of Nietzsche's philosophy was an attempt to find meaning within this given world and its many limitations.

Why Think with Friedrich

"When will Nietzsche explain something useful, like how to do a digital detox over a long holiday weekend and what craft beers I should drink while doing it?" you might be wondering at this point. Or perhaps you have more pointed concerns: "Wasn't Nietzsche some sort of proto-Nazi?" Call these the practical and the personal critiques. Both are worth engaging.

Pondering the value of an "easy life," considering ways to restrict our information intake, and finding strategies to increase immersion in local experiences do not sound as immediately useful as "Top Ten Tips for Taming Toxic Tech." Why are we talking about Dionysus and not a "no screens after 9:00 p.m." rule? What about a tasteful wicker basket placed beside the front door to collect devices as family members enter?

I have nothing against tasteful wicker baskets, but "practical" advice of this kind is wildly overrated. On a merely empirical level, hand-crafted receptacles have done little to halt our collective smartphone addiction. People pay ludicrous sums of money to go on "digital detox" vacations but immediately check their texts when the weekend's over. We must think more deeply about what we need from technology, information, and life itself. Only then can we formulate individual approaches that will last.

Case in point: the common claim that we need to "moderate" our screen time. *We spend far too much time staring at our screens*, the argument goes. *It's unhealthy! Let's cut back to a reasonable amount.* Well—sure. But if you are wasting 20 hours a week on useless screen time, cutting that number back to 10 hours a week means that you are still wasting 10 hours a week. This is certainly better, but it's hardly a goal in itself. What matters is *serving life*.

But few of us know ourselves as well as we imagine—in part because we don't have much time to really *think*. So we might reclaim that hour before dinner spent reading Reddit posts and instead flip through back issues of the *Economist* that are busy classing up the coffee table. (Do not underestimate just how virtuous this can feel!) But if we only use our newfound knowledge of Azerbaijani politics and the Scottish National Party to sound "well read," have we improved either our lives or the world? Or are we simply wasting time in a different way? Perhaps we can relate to Nietzsche's complaint in *Human, All Too Human*: "By an excess of effort [workers] win leisure for themselves, and then they can do nothing with it but count the hours until the tale is ended."

We simply do not know in advance that "moderating" screen time is a good in itself. If you're a novelist, staring at a monitor for 7 hours a day may be *exactly* what you need to achieve difficult, creative life goals. You might need more screen time in your life!

Or consider the claim that what we need, in our distracted, information-addled mental states, is "mindfulness." Nietzsche would love this, right? *We are immersing ourselves in the present!* But "fully experiencing the present moment" is, on its own, a good but limited value. In yoga classes, for instance, mindful breathing is often a calming and centering practice—which then rejuvenates us to resume our frenetic lives.

Mindfulness by itself does not answer the key questions: What moments should we most seek to *be present in*? And within those moments, what aspects of reality *should we be attending to*? And when we attend to them, are there some *we must seek to change*? These are, in a way, deeply moral questions, and many forms of attention will (or should) prompt us to action.

Alan Jacobs, a humanities professor at Baylor University, penned a provocative 2016 manifesto called "Attending to Technology: Theses for Disputation." Many of his theses concern the use and misuse of our attention. Jacobs lambasts "mindfulness" as a cure-all that too often devolves into "the cultivation of a mental stance without objects to attend to." In contrast, he argues, the "only mindfulness worth cultivating will be teleological through and through: it will be mindfulness *for* something—for personal formation, for service, for love."

This is thoroughly Nietzschean. Immersion in life—even in its earthiest physicality—matters, but never for its own sake. Our full engagement with life must be goal-oriented or else we float through time like tubers down a lazy river, coming to the end of our journey with nothing heroic or even all that interesting to show for it. As Nietzsche writes in *Thus Spoke Zarathustra:*

> I knew noble people who lost their highest hope. And then they slandered all high hopes. Then they lived churlishly in brief pleasures, scarcely casting their goals beyond the day . . . once they thought of becoming heroes: now they are libertines. To them the hero is grief and ghastliness. But by my love and hope I beseech you: do not throw away the hero in your soul!

Without a "highest hope" in the future, without a goal cast "beyond the day," mindfulness can devolve into an apolitical hedonism. Not even a Dionysian such as Nietzsche thinks that a good thing.

We need to go deeper than the facile wisdom our culture provides for dealing with our technological malaise. Tech tips and detox weekends aren't going to cut it. And we could do worse than spend a few hours in Nietzsche's company, thinking about the three areas we have discussed:

- an "easy life" that too often leaches our will to difficult goals;
- infinite information that overwhelms, distracts, and numbs;
- a constant stream of "elsewheres" that keeps us from full immersion in our own physical lives.

If those three issues still seem impractical, try thinking of them this way: Are they not the very promises made by Netflix, Google, and Facebook?

The dubious virtues of the "last man" resemble the virtues of technology itself, which is never neutral. Unless we provide countervailing goals of our own, technology will push us in the directions of its creators. How confident are we that today's high-tech overlords have the moral wisdom to shepherd our precious energy and attention toward the creation of our best lives?

To put it more crudely: Is Mark "Facebook" Zuckerberg really the guy you'd pick for a shaping role in your life story?

My own confidence in the technorati has been dropping. After years of writing about how the unsecured Internet has become a cesspool of fraud, spam, child pornography, government surveillance, invasive advertising, and racist chain emails from your uncle Fred, I am less convinced that the designers of our world-altering devices understand the world or the ways in which it should be altered. (I saw the brightest minds of our generation go to Facebook and Google, where they sold advertising.)

Lingering unease with my own digital utopia meant that I could still hear Nietzsche's warning *as* a warning. I became convinced that he is not necessarily someone to *agree with*—but that he might well be worth engaging.

Which brings us to more personal questions about who Nietzsche was and how far we want to walk his road. More than most philosophers, Nietzsche can be uncomfortable, disagreeable, "unsafe" to read. He constantly praises "warfare," valorizes "strength," and talks up the superhuman *übermensch*; all these themes would be linked with later Nazi ideology. His comments about women, especially in the latter half of his work, are of

almost no value whatsoever. And, in his late works, he occasionally says things like:

> The weak and ill-constituted shall perish: first principle
> of *our* philanthropy. And one shall help them to do so . . .

> The sick man is a parasite of society. In a certain state it
> is indecent to live longer. To go on vegetating in cow-
> ardly dependence on physicians and machinations, after
> the meaning of life, the right to life, has been lost, that
> ought to prompt a profound contempt in society. . . .
> Ascending life demands the most inconsiderate pushing
> down and aside of degenerating life—for example, for
> the right of procreation, for the right to be born, for the
> right to live.

Ugh. Take Nietzsche as your guru and you will run into all
sorts of problems. As one of my philosophy professors told me, "If
you're not offended by Nietzsche, you aren't paying attention."
Yet it may help to keep a few points in mind:

- Nietzsche's insanity was a process, not an event. Whatever caused it—doctors speculate endlessly in medical
  journals, even today—the disease seems to have pro-
  gressively lowered Nietzsche's mental modesty. In the
  last years of his sane life, his letters betray an increasing
  megalomania about his "destiny." Nietzsche's last few
  letters after his break are signed "Dionysus" or "The
  Crucified," and on his train journey back to an asylum,
  a friend records that he believed himself to be a king.
  Much in even his latest works remains valuable, but

the process of disease is worth keeping in mind when we recognize, for instance, that the two objectionable extracts above both come from the last months of his sane life.

• Nietzsche often speaks metaphorically. As we shall later see, most of his comments on war and cruelty and strength refer to intellectual and cultural battles—not to literal warfare. Context is crucial. Nietzsche was a relentless critic of German militarism after his own experiences in the cavalry and as a medic.

• Nietzsche "projects" wildly and obviously about many things. His comments about invalids, for instance, were written weeks before his own nervous collapse, which he had felt building for many years. He had spent much of his own life as an invalid who wore an eyeshade in public and whose digestion could handle only weak tea. This does not make his comments less disagreeable, although it might suggest that they are aspirational statements of what Nietzsche wanted for himself rather than a program of cruelty toward others.

• Nietzsche was no anti-Semite. He hated the German anti-Semites, including both the later Wagner and his sister Elisabeth's husband, Bernhard, a proto-fascist who killed himself upon the financial collapse of his racist colony in Paraguay. Weeks before his own collapse, Nietzsche wrote, "We can assent to no state of affairs which allows the canting bigot to be at the top." Even after his insanity, he kept up the theme; one of the few letters he sent before being bundled off to an asylum said, "I have just had all anti-Semites shot!"

• Nietzsche was no German nationalist. Christianity,

Socrates, Kant, Judaism, fellow scholars, and the late
Wagner all come in for plenty of abuse across Nietzsche's
corpus. But the greatest denunciations are reserved for
the contemporary German "culture" that Nietzsche
loathed, one that celebrated the emerging German *Reich*
and became increasingly nationalistic and warmongering.
Nietzsche instead styled himself a "good European."

- Nietzsche was a lonely and sick man who composed some
of the most beautiful German prose and the most provocative German philosophy while struggling even to read
and write. His eye pain, migraines, and bouts of vomiting were nearly incapacitating; he took (self-administered
and sometimes badly measured) sleeping draughts of
many kinds—which had their own horrific side effects.
Nietzsche is perhaps at his most moving when occasionally opening up about his weakness rather than projecting
a philosophy of "strength" and "health." While he would
have hated our pity, he might have accepted our respect
for the way he made his often wretched life into something productive and almost inspiring.

- Nietzsche was a bombastic exaggerator in print. In person, all accounts suggest he was a sober, courteous, soft-
spoken man who dressed conventionally and took care
over his personal grooming. But on the page, Nietzsche
unleashed words like volcanic explosions—powerful but
occasionally imprecise.

- Some of Nietzsche's ideas and arguments were simply
bad, cruel, or juvenile. But consider how unimpeachable
your own philosophical musings might have been at 27.
Most of Nietzsche's work was written in his twenties and
thirties; he went insane at 44.

In other words—Nietzsche was a flawed human being and a creature of his time. Modern critical introductions make this point clear. "There is plenty in each of these books to worry about and argue with, and much that is all-too-human in him no less than in his targets," writes Richard Schact in his introduction to *Human, All Too Human*.

"As always in reading Nietzsche, one needs to distinguish between the excited exaggeration even of so comparatively calm a work as *Daybreak*," writes Michael Tanner in his introduction to that book, "and the underlying genius of insight and prophecy which the exaggeration often conceals."

Oxford professor Bernard Williams uses his introduction to *The Gay Science* to lament Nietzsche's "recurrent weaknesses":

> There are cranky reflections on diet and climate. His opinions about women and sex, even if they include one or two shrewd and compassionate insights into the conventions of his time, are often shallow and sometimes embarrassing; they were, biographically, the product of an experience which had been drastically limited and disappointing. However, what is most significant for his thought as a whole is the fact that his resources for thinking about modern society and politics, in particular about the modern state, were very thin . . .

It was this last trait that made Nietzsche's work so amenable to groups such as the Nazis, because many groups could read themselves into Nietzsche's not-very-rigorous political views. This damaged his international reputation until some years after World War II had ended. Nietzsche was only rehabilitated in English by the eminent scholar and translator Walter Kaufmann, who nevertheless deplored Nietzsche's weaknesses: "bathos, sentences that invite quotation out of context in support of hideous causes, silly arguments."

But if you don't take Nietzsche as your guide and guru, if you instead embrace him as a dialogue partner and provocateur, these limitations need not be a roadblock to *thinking with him*. Nietzsche would have valued the attempt to wrestle with his ideas—even to reject some of them.

Nietzsche claimed to want no disciples, and he never provided a logical "system" of thought. He believed that forcing ideas into rigorous arrangements would necessarily lead the "systematizer" to falsify both thought and experience. "I mistrust all systematizers and avoid them," he writes in *Twilight of the Idols*. "The will to a system is a lack of integrity."

Nietzsche did, however, express a powerful vision of the good life. It is not a *system* and it is not a *program*. It has no "rules." It is a constellation of goals and values. Instead of tech-driven ease, Nietzsche says, we should embrace creative exertion. Instead of drowning beneath an infinite flood of content, we should seek deeper wisdom through careful curation and information restriction. Instead of a mental, screen-mediated existence, we should find more embodied immersion in the world.

This is not a Luddite vision of technology; it is about consolidating our gains while reckoning honestly with what we have lost. As Nietzsche puts it in a beautiful passage:

> We are faltering, but we must not let it make us afraid and perhaps surrender the new things we have gained. Moreover, we cannot return to the old, we have burned our boats; all that remains is for us to be brave, let hap-

pen what may.—Let us only go forward, let us only make a move!

Nietzsche will not leave you alone. To take him seriously is to face the possibility that you must remake yourself. You may need to say No to things that feel comfortable. You may need to say Yes to things that sound scary.

"There is no work of Nietzsche's that does not say to us," wrote Walter Kaufmann, "'You must change your life.'" But that is precisely why Nietzsche is such a potent person to *think with*.

Can a nineteenth-century German bachelor with a walrus mustache, a penchant for aphorism, and an aversion to alcohol really help us chart a course through our own tech-driven malaise? Reader, come and see.

Two

THE SECRET OF MY
HAPPINESS

A Yes, a No, a Straight Line, a Goal

WHAT A STRANGE URGE, THIS HUMAN NEED FOR PURPOSE.
Other animals lack it completely, while humans are driven mad
by meaning. Nietzsche says little about how this need might
have arisen in human prehistory, but he does speculate that
religious leaders and philosophers who taught a larger meaning
for our lives eventually kindled the concept within the broader
human family. Now we can't put their fire out.

"Human nature has on the whole been changed by the ever
new appearance of those teachers of the design of existence,"
Nietzsche writes in the very first section of *The Gay Science*, a
book about how to live joyfully in the absence of metaphysical
meaning. "Man has gradually become a visionary animal, who
has to fulfil one more condition of existence than the other
animals: man *must* from time to time believe that he knows
why he exists."

A key feature of Nietzsche's project was finding a way to
live in a world where divine purpose has been obliterated. We
might assume that Nietzsche would try to clear the lingering

underbrush of meaning that he found hiding everywhere—and that this project would end with him articulating a "post-purpose" way to live. But that's not what happens.

Nietzsche, all too human like the rest of us, craves meaning, even if he must provide it for himself. Perhaps because his lifelong illness deprived him of so many common pleasures—sleep, sex, food, the simple feeling of robust good health—Nietzsche could not content himself with hedonism. If life's meaning was pleasure, it remained out of reach; indeed, a life of mere ease becomes the hallmark of the "last man."

Nietzsche needed a goal, and he attributed some of his own sickness to the lack of direction he felt after he resigned his post at Basel. Ill and jobless, his search for meaning took on a passion and intensity seen most often in the religious life that he disdained. What he needed most, he realized, was not an end to suffering; he needed a journey and a destination.

"We thirsted for lightning and action, of all things we kept ourselves furthest from the happiness of the weaklings, from 'resignation,'" he writes of himself at this time. "There was a thunderstorm in our air, the nature which we are grew dark—*for we had no road*. Formula of our happiness: a Yes, a No, a straight line, a *goal*."

The message here, expressed with all the drama of a teenager's diary entry, might sound banal: meaning matters. But Nietzsche never claimed that his call to live a goal-oriented life was novel—only that we so easily lose sight of what matters.

As he wrote in *Human, All Too Human*, a book he later called his monument to crisis:

In a journey, we commonly forget its goal. Almost every vocation is chosen and entered upon as means to an end,

but is continued as the ultimate end. Forgetting our purpose is the most frequent form of folly.

Nietzsche's own experience as a prodigy, pushed into a career
suited to his talents but not his deepest needs, made him keenly
aware of how *lesser goals* impress themselves upon us. We may
absorb them from our community without conscious reflection,
even when they run against the grain of our deeper desires.

This is why a discussion about the role technology plays in
our lives cannot begin with questions about screen time, too
much "blue light" before bed, or how many text messages we
send or receive daily. We start instead at the level of our fundamental life goals—and decide if they have been too influenced
by the post–Industrial Revolution emphasis on safety, ease, control, leisure, abundance, connection, and health.

For Nietzsche, we have been so influenced, and the effects
are both pernicious and invisible. We never filled out a card asking us if we *wanted* to watch 5 hours of video content a day; it
just sort of . . . happened. And it felt good. We became the "last
man" without any single decision to do so.

For Nietzsche, ranking comfort too highly can dampen our
desire to strive, to risk, and to create, these more difficult goals
that matter to living a fully orbed human life. The safety, the
ease, the astonishing control we have over everything from our
temperature to our TV programming, the leisure time that has
become its own kind of performance, the information abundance, our global and instantaneous connections, and our long-
lived healthiness—these should all be means, not ends.

This does not mean that Nietzsche values every kind of hard
work or the striving that becomes mere workaholism or wealth-
gathering. Nietzsche disliked work that saps the human spirit,

that offers no creativity and no scope for skill, that offers us only the "small goals," the easy life. This kind of work can numb the individual spirit. As Nietzsche writes in *Daybreak*:

> For at the sight of work—that is to say, severe toil from morning till night—we have the feeling that it is the best police—that it holds every one in check and effectively hinders the development of reason, of greed, and of desire for independence. For work uses up an extraordinary proportion of nervous force, withdrawing it from reflection, meditation, dreams, cares, love, and hatred; it dangles unimportant aims before the eyes of the worker and affords easy and regular gratification.

Thus it happens that a society where work is continually being performed will enjoy greater security, and it is security that is now venerated as the supreme deity.

Such work leads only to exhaustion. As Stanford professor Robert McGinn puts it in an essay on Nietzsche's technological views, "Leisure in the age of work is not a time of life-affirming creativity and renewal but one of 'letting go' and of crude stretching out 'as long and wide and ungainly as one happens to be.'"

In our day, technology plays a key role in both workaholism and hedonism. Through email, texting, cell phones, and the Internet, we can work from anywhere at any time. The recent global pandemic showed many knowledge workers the freedom that can come from working at home, but it also reminded us of the burnout that arises from being always available for yet another videoconference. At the same time, every moment of downtime now has us reaching for our phones or our television remotes. Screens are how we work and how we relax.

This technological ubiquity explains why our digital tools so easily trigger those internal warnings that something is wrong. Existential crisis can provoke change, but we can't hear the alarm if we constantly dampen the drumbeat of dissatisfaction.

As Nietzsche's own case reminds us, the experience of "waking up" from your own life to realize that you aren't living it as you want is a common one. No text messaging addiction or "lost weekends" of Netflix bingeing are required to keep us from thinking too hard about our situation—but they certainly work, because our technologies provide endless stimulation. And we crave that stimulation above all else.

Humans have long sought to be, in T.S. Eliot's well-known phrase, "distracted from distraction by distraction / Filled with fancies and empty of meaning." But our need to feel *anything* is now nearly pathological. We long for distraction so much that we would rather feel shocks over silence.

In a 2014 study, researchers from Harvard and the University of Virginia teamed up for an experiment in which participants experienced several stimuli, from pretty pictures to an electric shock. They were then asked how much money they would pay to have or to avoid that experience again. Those who said they would pay money to avoid being shocked more were placed in an unadorned room and left alone for 15 minutes. They were told to "entertain themselves with their thoughts." If they *wanted* to do so, they were told, they could also zap themselves with an electric current; all it took was a button press. According to the study, "67 percent of men (12 of 18) gave themselves at least one shock during the thinking period," though there was one outlier who "administered 190 shocks to himself." Among women, 25 percent pressed the shock button.

The authors concluded: "What is striking is that simply being alone with their own thoughts for 15 min[utes] was apparently so aversive that it drove many participants to self-administer an electric shock that they had earlier said they would pay to avoid."

To reflect wisely on our lives instead of just soaking up the values of a tech-driven society, we must reduce this need for stimulation. If we can find the time and space to reflect on the purpose and meaning of our lives, we can better control technology so that it will serve our goals rather than reinforce our frenzy.

But what exactly is a "Nietzschean" goal?

Truths That Cut into Our Flesh Like Knives

Nietzsche has nothing to say to the efficiency-minded self-help crowd; he has few practical ideas for ordering a day or a season or a year. This is just as well, given Nietzsche's eccentricities; such tips from him would largely boil down to musings about avoiding electrical storms, finding a dry Italian climate that isn't too cold in the winter, and dosing oneself with sleeping draughts and stimulants.

Nietzsche does like to talk about goals, though, and when he does so, he is talking about the most basic use of our vital energies. A well-lived life embraces unceasing creative struggle and acknowledges human limitation but still strives for excellence.

In a passage from one of his notebooks, published after his death, Nietzsche writes eloquently about this need for goals:

> If the "why" of one's life is clear, then the "how" will take care of itself. It is already a sign of doubt in the "why," in the purpose and meaning of life, indeed, a sign

of a lack of will, when the value of pleasure and pain come to the fore, when hedonistic and pessimistic teachings find a sympathetic ear. Renunciation, resignation, virtue, "objectivity": these may be signs that the absence of the most important factor, the ability to set goals for oneself, is already beginning to be felt.

Here are five questions that help us think through what Nietzsche meant.

IS MY GOAL *POSITIVE*?

Nietzsche did not believe that negative goals—don't do this, tear down that—were ultimate. He suspected that negative goals were too limited to be of much real good, so he demanded "positive" activity, a vision that calls us forward into a new reality.

"At bottom, I find those moral codes distasteful which say: 'Do not do this! Renounce! Overcome yourself!' " he writes in *The Gay Science*. So far, so expected. But then comes this riff from the great "immoralist":

> On the other hand, I am in favor of those moral codes which urge me to do something again and again, from morning till evening, to dream of it at night, to think of nothing but: do this well, do this as only I can, and to the best of my ability.

In *Zarathustra*, writing in his faux-prophetic style, Nietzsche makes the same point about morality requiring positive, not negative, feelings. "Ever since there have been human beings, they have enjoyed themselves too little," says Zarathustra. "That alone, my brothers, is our original sin! And if we learn to enjoy ourselves better, so do we best unlearn our hurting of others and our planning hurts for them."

Nietzsche isn't amoral—he simply believes that negative morality is, in a word, *too easy*. We need something that calls for our striving, not just our renunciation.

This attitude agrees with Nietzsche's more general conception of "the will to power." Even if you know nothing of Nietzsche, you have heard the phrase. It sounds like a totalitarian motto—and Nietzsche has been smeared as a proto-Nazi because of it. But Nietzsche is the great prophet of the *individual*, and what he has in mind with the "will to power" is not crude domination over others but the *ascending vitality of life itself*. The "will to power" is the evolutionary pressure to exert ourselves in the world, to leave a mark, to create and to reproduce.

Every creature, Nietzsche argues, "instinctively strives for an optimum of favorable conditions under which it can expend all its strength and achieve its maximal feeling of power; every animal abhors . . . every kind of intrusion or hindrance that obstructs or could obstruct this path to the optimum." This "optimum" need not involve "pleasure"; in fact, Nietzsche claims that pursuit of the optimum often leads to unhappiness. The optimum is about the "path to power, to action, to the most powerful activity."

This need to take positive action is more primal than pleasure. It is more primal than survival. That is because humans do not aim directly at life or at pleasure but "at the extension of power," even though this "often enough calls in question self-preservation and sacrifices it." This is precisely "the will to power, which is just the will to live."

This will to power is neither *good* nor *evil*. (Remember that Nietzsche is the author of a book called *Beyond Good and Evil*;

he wants to show how ideas work in the world, before we apply value labels.) Nietzsche's excavations of human behavior are provocative and often fascinating, such as when he shows how the "will to power" might explain even the "powerless" phenomenon of asceticism; here the feeling of power is directed inward, with the goal of self-mastery or self-mortification. While our need to feel power might explain the pleasure human societies have taken in public executions, it also drives the skilled trades, the arts, and our inventors.

In his book *The World Beyond Your Head*, Matthew Crawford explores the link between this "will to power" and human skill. "Friedrich Nietzsche said that joy is the feeling of one's power increasing," Crawford writes.

> It captures something important about the role that skill plays in a good life. When we become competent in some skilled action, the very elements of the world that were initially sources of frustration become elements of a self that has expanded, by analogy with the way a toddler expands into his own body and comes to inhabit it comfortably. And this feels good.

We can turn the "will to power" this way and that, inward and outward, toward cruelty or creativity, but we cannot turn it off. Turning it off is to embrace death. If we do, we will give in to the nihilism that ultimately leads to despair. Built for positive action, we must create positive goals.

IS MY GOAL *CREATIVE*?

Truly meaningful action in the world is, in Nietzsche's view, *creative action*—and he grounds this assertion in biology.

Evolutionary thought dominated Nietzsche's time. Though he disagreed with Darwin on certain fundamental interpretations of the evolutionary process, Nietzsche saw in evolution a powerful explanation for human behavior. And if life evolved through struggle, growing ever more prodigally diverse as the millennia ticked on, then creative struggle becomes not just a matter of "artistic temperament" but a bedrock principle of existence.

Does technology help or hinder such goals? Given that science and technology have radically remade the post-Enlightenment world, this is no idle question. Looking around at German and English society, in particular, Nietzsche had to concede that his age was one of creative mechanical invention. He is clear in *Human, All Too Human* that technology is "a product of the highest intellectual energies" and that it "releases a vast quantity of energy in general that would otherwise lie dormant."

Machines can free us from drudgery, but these unlocked energies are always at risk of waste. When they don't encourage human creativity, machines re-create humanity in their own image: active but uncreative, powerful but identical. Humans, and our work, become commodities.

Nietzsche already saw this happening around him, through factory work in particular. Too many of the "energies" unleashed by industrial machines are "the lower, unthinking forces" of our natures. Such work "does not communicate the impulse to climb higher, to improve, to become artistic. It creates activity and monotony, but this in the long-run produces a counter-effect, a despairing ennui of the soul, which through machinery has learnt to hanker after the variety of leisure."

Nietzsche loved hard work but hated the cult of productivity. His critique of idleness here is not a call to work *more*; it is a call for creative labor and renewing rest. In the lifestyles of factory workers he saw long and boring work, which then turned leisure hours into a quest for simple relaxation or stimulation.

A leisure-work paradigm like this is not going to produce the *übermensch*. Nietzsche worries that "the proliferation of intriguing technological innovations will enhance the esteem of the merely novel while distracting attention from and diminishing respect for the truly creative," McGinn writes. "Neither of these cultural changes will contribute to the enhancement of human development." Thus we have the irony of humanity's creations sapping humanity of creativity, turning us into the "last man."

This doesn't have to happen, though. Technology is an outcome of the "will to power," and it distills human desire for skill, mastery, and invention into mechanical or digital form. Like the will to power, it is neither good nor bad.

We may use our technological tools to live more creatively. I look back with fondness at the many childhood hours I spent coding primitive computer games on an Atari 600XL. Simple as the final product was, the problem-solving, the logic, the memorization required to master a programming language mesmerized me. I was at once both a technology user (of the computer and the BASIC programming language) and a technology creator (my new piece of computer code, complete with inelegant subroutines and 8-bit graphics). And when the program ran successfully for the first time, I didn't care to play it; I wanted immediately to *improve* it. This was technology experienced as a spur to creation and invention.

Nietzsche himself deeply loved the piano, which he played with real *Sturm und Drang* energy. Though we take it for granted, the modern piano is a complex invention stuffed with strings, pedals, hammers, and keys; it relies on tempered tuning systems developed over centuries and can, unlike the harpsichord, vary its volume dramatically. Building one requires wood- and metalworking skill, maintaining one requires regular tuning, and playing one demands two-handed mastery of complex polyphonic tones. It is a device only possible to build after the development of numerous underlying craft techniques and musical theorizing, and it is relatively new in human history. Nietzsche found great joy both in composing and playing on the instrument, and it was one of the important ways that he wove music into his life.

Because technology can empower so many human ends, from war to industrial production to science to art, Nietzsche was ultimately conflicted about it. "The development and use of certain technologies offer opportunities for strengthening the active, creative side of human nature, something vital to Nietzsche's ideal of human life," McGinn notes.

> On the other hand, many technologies, especially in modern society, have effects which engender or reinforce inertial behavior in their users. Thus Nietzsche deplored the fact that factory work dissipated much of the energy of workers, some of which might, perhaps with the aid of other technologies, be liberated and utilized for creative ends.

The question for us to ask is whether the goals we set ourselves are both positive and creative—and if so, whether our technology usage patterns help us get there.

DOES MY GOAL *MATTER*?
It is not difficult to imagine a life spent in service of something positive, creative, but utterly trivial. (My conversations with

former digital advertising execs suggest that the industry is rife with examples.) Nietzsche promotes goals that *matter*, and he sets the bar high for what this means. Ease and security are not enough. They may be adjuncts to various goals, but the goals themselves are things that we *must* seek or die in attempting. (So, not digital advertising campaigns.)

Here's how Nietzsche talks about truths that matter in *Daybreak*:

> We all live, comparatively speaking, in far too great security for us ever to acquire a sound knowledge of man: one person studies him from a desire to do so, another from boredom, a third from habit: it is never a case of: "study or perish!" As long as truths do not cut into our flesh with knives, we retain a secret contempt for them.

Isn't this a bit . . . dramatic? Certainly. But Nietzsche's own life goal was the discovery and creation of meaning in a world where metaphysical ideas about God and "purpose" had broken down. The result of this collapse, Nietzsche worried as he looked around the wreckage of his own life, was *nihilism*. (Note: Whenever you come across one of the many references to Nietzsche as a "nihilist," you know that the author has no idea what he or she is talking about.) Humans require purpose. This was a truth that cut into Nietzsche's own flesh like a blade; the pain of it was intolerable. In those passages where Nietzsche believes he has solved the problem of purpose, you can feel the joy radiating from the page. It was a drama that he lived.

Without taking time to face such questions about their goals, the "active" members of society may never find deserving targets for their vital energies. Instead, they get caught up in society's goals, which do not necessarily mean anything.

"It is the misfortune of active men that their activity is almost always a bit irrational," Nietzsche writes. "For example, one must not inquire of the money-gathering banker what the purpose for his restless activity is: it is irrational. Active people roll like a stone, conforming to the stupidity of mechanics."

He goes on:

> For lack of rest, our civilization is turning into a new barbarism. At no period have the active, that is, the restless, been of *more* importance. One of the necessary corrections, therefore, which must be undertaken in the character of humanity is to strengthen the contemplative element on a large scale.

This "contemplative element" may conjure up silent retreat weekends in a Catskills ashram, eating too much tempeh and meditating on The Meaning of Life. For some, this is indeed creative, renewing bliss. For others, it's a recipe for dull earnestness.

And yet, so convinced of his own meaningful work that he could write an autobiographical chapter called "Why I Am a Destiny," Nietzsche does not equate "meaning" with "seriousness." He is not one of those world-changing visionaries who can never tell a joke. For Nietzsche, the person acting out a meaningful goal should have *light feet*, become a *dancer*, learn to *defy gravity*, and, most of all—learn to feel *better joys*.

IS MY GOAL *EXCELLENCE*?

Stay with me here: The idea that you should aim for "excellence" may *not* come across as life-altering advice from the mind of our mustachioed German. My mother, for instance, who never read a word of Nietzsche, repeatedly told me that "anything worth doing is worth doing well." This applied especially to our gargantuan garden, where I spent many hours as a kid sitting on an overturned bucket and wondering just how badly I could weed the carrots and not be sent back to do it again.

But Nietzsche's concern with excellence takes a somewhat different form. It is not quite "anything worth doing is worth doing well"; it is more like "a person living well does not settle for ease alone but struggles with the world in the pursuit of excellence."

This is one reason Nietzsche hates cultural conformity. To him, it looks like a straitjacket that keeps people from embracing their own unique excellences. That attitude explains blistering quotes like this one, from *Twilight of the Idols*:

> The man *who has become free*—and how much more the
> *mind* that is become free—spurns the contemptible sort
> of well-being dreamed of by shopkeepers, Christians,
> cows, women, Englishmen and other democrats. The
> free man is a *warrior*.

Nietzsche's list of targets here is eclectic and objectionable, but his point is simple: Conformity, tradition, safety, and ease are "herd" virtues that can constrain the free spirit. That spirit is here described as a warrior, not because Nietzsche enjoyed war but because he admired the attitude of the ancient Greeks, who saw life as a constant struggle (*agon*) in the pursuit of excellence (*arete*).

It's hard to convey how much this child of the nineteenth century saw his world through the lens of ancient Greece. It was, frankly, a little weird; Basel, Naumburg, and Schulpforta had about as much in common with Periclean Athens as I have with a naked mole rat.

Nietzsche marinated himself in a worldview that valued

struggle above everything. To struggle—and to come out on top—was the mark of a winner. Those who avoid the *agon* are members of the "herd." They have given up on excellence as a cardinal virtue in life, and they have traded it for ease. Humans need instead to become adventurers, even *warriors*.

"Nietzsche did not intend to prescribe warfare, or even individual combat, as the 'healthiest' human activity," writes Princeton professor Paul Zweig. "He meant to offer combat as a model for the more complex activities of culture. . . . He meant to propose an agonistic vision of culture, and of life itself."

This sheds more light on a quote from *Zarathustra*:

> To modestly embrace a small happiness—that they call "resignation" and already they are squinting around modestly for a new small happiness. At bottom these simple ones want one simple thing: that no one harm them. . . . You are becoming smaller and smaller, you small people! You are crumbling, you contented ones! You will yet perish—of your many small virtues, of your many small abstentions, of your many small resignations! Too sparing, too yielding—that is your soil! But in order for a tree to grow *tall*, it needs to put down hard roots amid hard rock!

For Nietzsche, struggle is not incidental to excellence; it is *absolutely necessary* for it. This explains why his contempt for "ease" is tied to the idea of *becoming great*.

DOES MY GOAL *OVERCOME ITSELF*?

Continual struggle carries a final implication for Nietzschean goals—they are never static. Nietzsche, the great philosopher of flux and "becoming," does not endorse a fixed version of excellence, a moment when one "arrives." There are always mountains beyond mountains.

In Nietzschean terms, this is a *continual overcoming*. We see this clearly in art, where mastering a particular style is often the very moment at which an artist attempts something new. Nietzsche wants nothing to do with the static excellence of the painter who masters pictures of cozy winter chalets and spends the next 40 years churning out more for tourists. Instead, Nietzsche encourages a restless human urge to push through boundaries, to pause only long enough to gather energy for the next expedition. As Zarathustra puts it:

> And this secret life itself spoke to me: "Behold," it said, "I am *that which must always overcome itself*. . . . Whatever I may create and however I may love it—soon I must oppose it and my love, thus my will wants it."

Excellence, for Nietzsche, always pushes further.

The Slopes of Vesuvius

This more adventurous and creative approach to life has a downside: danger.

Modern technology has given us such increased control—over travel, disease, temperature, the height of our grass, when we watch TV shows, who we encounter, how we arrange words—that we expect it. And modern regulatory states incrementally reduce risk, patching up aircraft vulnerabilities after every crash and issuing detailed guidelines about the distance between crib slats.

Lower risk and greater control intoxicate us. Together, they breed cultures of safety, where setbacks look more like failures of planning than unavoidable consequences of risking ourselves to an uncontrollable world. The recent global pandemic has reminded us all just how deeply such a feeling of safety runs in many parts of the world—especially when it comes to contagious disease. Thankfully, technology saved millions of lives by enabling remote work, videoconferencing, genetic sequencing, and vaccine development, but there were months in which the ephemeral nature of human life was brought home anew even to the powerful.

Safety through technology is no bad thing—Nietzsche himself sought doctors and medicines throughout his life—but it can become pathological. It too easily convinces us that such safety is an ultimate condition. Soon enough, relinquishing control so that we might take on risky ventures feels foolish or even impossible. Simply leaving our homes can become a challenge.

One does not have to read far in the literature on technology to find this point made in stark terms. Two recent examples could stand in for many more.

San Diego State University professor Jean Twenge has spent years researching young people's technology habits. She calls those coming of age over the past decade "iGen," because they grew up with digital tools such as the iPhone, and she has collected huge amounts of data on them. Her conclusion is clear:

> The strongest legacy of iGen'ers' involvement in the online world may be their increased physical safety. They are spending more time on their phones and computers and less time driving and seeing their friends in person, and as a result their physical safety has reached unprec-

edented levels. They are less willing to take chances, and their definition of safety has expanded to include their emotions as well as their bodies. The more they use words to communicate, the less they put their bodies at risk and the more they put their emotions at risk.

Sherry Turkle, the MIT researcher, has reached similar conclusions. Rather than take risks in the broader world, digital technology in particular has taught us to stay immobile, using our words and images to reach out through screens. Turkle writes movingly of ways in which teenagers and college students remain "tethered" to parents through near-constant texting and phone calls, which can make it harder to take the small daily risks that teach independence.

> Our networked life allows us to hide from each other, even as we are tethered to each other. We'd rather text than talk. . . . Today, our machine dream is to be never alone but always in control. This can't happen when one is face-to-face with a person.

These are hardly attitudes that encourage wild risk-taking. As a parent myself, I'm okay with this, but such attitudes can also discourage *reasonable and necessary* risk-taking.

Nietzsche saw this worship of safety in much of the middle- and upper-class life of Europe, and he assailed it. He does not go as far as Jesus, who said that one must lose one's life in order to truly find it, but Nietzsche does think we must be *willing* to do so. In *The Gay Science,* published a few years after his decision to resign the only real job he would ever hold, he reflects on what he has learned:

For—believe me—the secret for harvesting from existence the greatest fruitfulness and the greatest enjoyment
is—to live dangerously! Build your cities on the slopes
of Vesuvius! Send your ships into uncharted seas! Live at
war with your peers and yourselves! Be robbers and con-
querors as long as you cannot be rulers and possessors,
you seekers of knowledge! Soon the time will be past in
which you had to be content living hidden in forests like
shy deer!

Given the uses to which Nietzsche has been put in the past,
one cannot say too many times that this is not a call to become
a thug, an invader, or a Jerky McJerkface. The "war" is directed
at oneself; the robbing and conquering is addressed to "seekers
of knowledge." It is a call to freedom and fearlessness, not to
petty larceny.

Such action is risky. We may anger others. We may fail ourselves. We might even lose our lives. But a risky death may be
preferable to a drawn-out life, as Nietzsche says in *Daybreak*:

And if you must perish, then do so immediately and suddenly; for in that case you will perhaps leave proud ruins
behind you! and not, as is now to be feared, merely mole-
hills, covered with grass and weeds.

Nietzsche's basic premise: *Failure is an option.* It is the necessary correlate of living the kind of life worth living, of having
the kind of goal worth having.

For those raised in the religion of success, accepting this possible outcome can be difficult. Success appears as a matter of life
and death. It is *serious.* But Nietzsche argues that the creative,

meaningful, and successful life is ultimately a kind of game. In this vision, failure offers the chance to laugh, to reset the pieces, and to play another round.

> Shy, ashamed, awkward, like the tiger whose spring has failed—thus, you higher men, have I often seen you slink aside. A *cast* which you made had failed. But what does it matter, you dice-players! You had not learned to play and joke as one must play and joke! Do we not ever sit at a great table of joking and playing? And if great things have been a failure with you, have you yourselves there-fore—been a failure? . . . Be of good cheer; what does it matter? How much is still possible! Learn to laugh at yourselves, as you ought to laugh!

We have heard this theme before, in another key. Though safety, comfort, and ease are not bad things, they can keep us from the striving that Nietzsche prefers.

> He who has always much indulged himself sickens at last by his over-indulgence. Praises on what makes hardy! I do not praise the land where butter and honey flow! To learn to look away from oneself is necessary in order to see many things:—this hardiness is needed by every mountain climber.

Or, to put it another way, the "last man" is not much of an adventurer.

For Nietzsche, adventure must be a lifestyle, not a week-end activity. We cannot actually know the world, nor can we know the passions that animate our own lives, by simply sitting and *thinking*. We cannot look inward, like Descartes, and find ground truth through mental activity alone. We gain the deep wisdom of life only through *experience*. As Paul Zweig puts it in a passage on Nietzsche and adventure:

> Repeatedly [Nietzsche] insists that "knowledge" cannot be obtained through Cartesian detachment. The philosopher who shuts out all of his senses and meditates in the darkness of his intellect may discover that he thinks and therefore is. . . . But how much closer will he then be to understanding the drives of nature, and of human nature?

Consider for a moment Nietzsche's style. For a philosopher, his writing is hyperbolic, colorful, and action-oriented—almost as though it comes from a comic book or an adventure novel. This can come across as juvenile. But the point of it seems to be that Nietzsche wants to *enact* through prose what his pen preaches.

"In order to make this point," Zweig says, "Nietzsche was not content simply to argue, although he does so often and well." Instead, "he created a stylistic medium, using the language of epic and high adventure, which the novel had relegated to the badlands of popular literature, in order to dramatize the agonistic quality of knowledge, his view that intelligence without courage or willpower was not attuned to the energies of life, and therefore could make only pale discoveries."

If anything about this conception of life sounds right, then it may be time to take a personal inventory. Which of our devices and practices enable a life that experiences the world in ways and places not always engineered for our comfort? Which bits of technology do we need to strip away in order to risk ourselves in ways that can help us to grow?

A Vision for Everyone?

All this "eye of the tiger" stuff about grabbing life by the horns, launching from the couch to become an adventurer—it has a dark side. And we need to face up to it before deciding if we can proceed.

Nietzsche likes to look down on people. For a middle-class kid from a pastor's family in an unremarkable German town, our philosopher imbibed a shocking level of aristocratic sentiment. You may have glimpsed it in his earlier dismissal of "women" and "democrats" and "shopkeepers" and "Christians" (and, um, the English).

In an aristocratic society, orders of rank exist everywhere, especially in human relations. Those higher on the scale of social value look down on their inferiors. For Nietzsche, this is no bad thing, and it is one reason why his metaphors so often involve altitude: living on the heights, dancing in the mountains, leaping from glacier to glacier.

For Nietzsche, looking down on people can teach us to feel a sensation of "distance" within our own souls—the gap between "us" and "them." After identifying this sensation, we may want to increase it by boosting our own "height." This process of recognizing hierarchies and leaping toward the top of them can create a certain kind of genius; that is, it can set people on the striving and struggling path to becoming the *übermensch*. (This is explicitly stated in section 257 of *Beyond Good and Evil*.)

Nietzsche's ethics and politics are aristocratic rather than democratic because he believes that equality works as a leveling principle on human society. Nietzsche, arch-individualist, sees the cultivation of exceptional human specimens as more important than anything that might happen to the general "herd" of humanity.

> Their song of "equal rights," "free society," "no longer either lords or slaves," does not allure us! We do not by any means think it desirable that the kingdom of righteousness and peace should be established on earth (because under any circumstances it would be the kingdom of the profoundest mediocrity . . .); we rejoice in all men, who, like ourselves, love danger, war, and adventure, who do not make compromises, nor let themselves be captured, conciliated, and stunted; we count ourselves among the conquerors.

If you think this sounds like a quote from the *Jerkwad Manifesto*, you're not alone. Nietzsche does admit that not hurting and exploiting one another "may in a certain rough sense become good manners between individuals if the conditions for it are present (namely if their strength and value standards are in fact similar)." But to make even something so apparently unobjectionable into a basic social principle such as the Golden Rule is, in his view, to make your will equal to another's. For Nietzsche, giving up one's individual will is a great sin. It amounts to "the will to the *denial* of life, as the principle of dissolution and decay."

These ideas about value, power, and will permeate Nietzsche's work. They form the basis of his "master" and "slave" moralities, in which the powerful take affirmative actions and declare them good—while the powerless respond by creating virtues through resentment, subterfuge, and negation. Nietzsche doesn't always take sides here—he claims to be explaining the origins of different value systems, not necessarily weighing them—but readers have long felt that he leans hard toward the "masters." Certainly, master morality more easily maps the characteristics of Nietzschean goals.

The scholarly debate around these issues bangs and clatters on. It may never be settled. But Nietzsche says enough objectionable things about human value and equality that you can reasonably wonder if his most interesting ideas can be decoupled from his most retrograde.

Is Nietzsche's "a Yes, a No, a straight line, a goal" rhetoric inspiration only for the powerful and privileged? Does it encompass more than the creative class—artists and coders—to include manual laborers, the poor, and those with disabilities? Does his "live like a robber!" rhetoric offer more than the sex, drugs, and rock 'n' roll approach to life? Or is all this inspiring talk just a license for narcissists to leave children and spouses behind in order to "follow their dreams"?

There's more to Nietzsche than this, but these are real dangers to keep in mind. Taking his points in their cheapest or most literal senses will not always increase human flourishing.

But we ought not dismiss Nietzsche's interest in active creative excellence as something befitting only, say, "creatives." Nietzsche's examples throughout his books are often drawn from factory workers. I think we lack creativity of our own if we can't see the ways his call toward goal-driven living might be possible for most of us.

These lives may not resemble what Nietzsche himself would have envisioned, but that seems fine when talking about a thinker who *wanted no disciples*. Active creative excellence isn't just the province of artists such as Wagner; a truly creative family life, for instance, or making space for writing and music requires no higher station.

We can reject Nietzsche's aristocratic rhetoric while still accepting the value in much of what he has to say, including his call to discover new and creative possibilities for being human. We can figure those possibilities in many ways. Nietzsche's rhetoric skews violent, but nonviolent leaders such as Martin Luther King, Jr., Desmond Tutu, and Mohandas Gandhi have arguably been some of the most creative, goal-driven, and *effective* leaders of the past hundred years.

Nietzsche may not have meant to include everyone, but even those he might have excluded can still learn from him.

Do We Really Know Ourselves?

Perhaps our discussion so far has triggered an itch at the back of your brain.

"Life is not just about ease," you might think with approval. "Life is instead about difficult but joyful work in the service of creative, active, meaningful, excellent, and self-overcoming goals. Absolutely! Where can I subscribe to this man's newsletter?"

But after spending 10 minutes blissed out in the bathtub, pondering these creative goals while listening to Survivor's greatest hits on repeat, that niggling itch might return. Can we really conjure up Nietzschean life goals by simply *thinking* about them with some quality 1980s hair metal playing in the background?

After all, knowing ourselves is difficult, and we can never peer inward unshaped by the world in which we have been raised. In societies that have become relentlessly technological, this shaping is significant—and it goes well beyond individual ideas and choices. We are shaped not just by evolution and by family, but by a relentlessly technological culture.

Karl Marx saw that technologies, though they may be bent to individual uses, also exert broader social effects. "The windmill gives you society with the feudal lord," he wrote in *The Poverty of Philosophy*. "The steam-mill, society with the industrial capitalist."

In *Technopoly*, Neil Postman echoes Marx's point. "Embedded in every tool is an ideological bias," he writes, "a predisposition to construct the world as one thing rather than another, to value one thing over another, to amplify one sense or skill or attitude more loudly than another."

Or as Nietzsche himself puts it: "The press, the machine, the railway, the telegraph are premises whose thousand-year conclusion no one has yet dared to draw."

Technology does not simply alter the societies in which we live; it makes certain life possibilities easier to imagine—and others much harder to entertain. When we try to craft goals for our own lives, we do so from within a society that has already sketched its preferences on the canvas of our lives.

Yes, "technology" writ large is a tool, and tools can be put to many ends. Give someone a shovel and they can either dig a basement or commit a murder; give someone a smartphone and they can connect with family members five states away or drown themselves in the most dehumanizing forms of pornography.

But saying that technology can be turned to many ends is not the same as saying that it turns toward all ends with the same ease. A new technology often interacts with human desires to produce *unintended consequences*.

When I was in college, a friend of mine spent his evenings logged into our campus Unix server, where he ran the text-based program called "ychat" that allowed him to have typewritten but real-time conversations with a girlfriend in Arizona. (Though it may be hard to remember now, this was important because long-distance phone calls were expensive.) They eventually got married.

Meanwhile, I was looking for love in all the wrong places—specifically, in IT data closets. There, I could snatch an hourly respite from my actual campus computing job and fire up a dumb terminal to check my text-based Unix email client "pine" for messages from A Woman I Fancied But Who Did Not Like Me In "That Way" (AWIFBWDNLMITW). I and AWIFBWDN-LMITW did *not* get married.

We used these Unix-based chat and email clients because they tapped into the basic human desire for connection, making it easier, cheaper, and faster than before. The goals behind these early programs were collaborative, research-oriented, and non-commercial. Their creators did not want to soak up our attention, nor did anyone want to sell you anything. The code itself was free.

Yet email and chat quickly escaped academia and invaded the corporate campus, eventually turning many knowledge workers into "email answering services" who could only get more tangible work done when they stopped replying to messages. With the rise of home Internet access and then the smartphone, these tools followed employees out of the office, then colonized their homes and tagged along on vacation.

Email and chat are largely the same products they were 30 years ago. They did not need to be specially engineered to hook our attention; they simply accelerated the connective possibilities of older inventions such as the telephone and the postal service. We loved them, and we used them—and eventually, they changed how and where we work. This can be hugely positive, enabling remote work during the recent pandemic and cutting down on all the time spent and pollution emitted by commuting. They can also be negative, making it simple to do even more work than before and making it difficult to ever be truly out of office. Our own goals may never have included "answering work emails on Sunday nights," but here we are.

Other technologies, though, have the *fully intended goal* of ensnaring our attention. Many modern digital services want to monopolize human attention; making money, so the thinking goes, is simple once you have a billion people using your product.

People outside the technology world are often surprised to learn how much research and engineering goes into making modern digital technology compelling. It has literally become a science at places such as Stanford University's Persuasive Tech Lab, where the goal is to engineer "machines designed to change humans." And companies such as Netflix spend liberally on making their services addictive; in 2009, the company handed out a $1 million prize to an outside research team that improved the Netflix recommendation algorithm by only 10 percent. Cal Newport, the computer scientist, puts it this way: "People don't succumb to screens because they're lazy, but instead because billions of dollars have been invested to make this outcome inevitable."

Through both unintended effects and intended goals, our technology does not simply sit silent, waiting to serve. It points us in various directions. It favors certain choices. It creates new possibilities. Taken together, technology's total effects shape the kinds of lives we can imagine.

Yes, personal choices matter. We can use Facebook only in ways and for amounts of time that we think appropriate, but our exercise of choice takes place within the confines of a service engineered to exploit our evolutionary wiring. We can choose differently, but as repeated research has shown, exerting willpower wears us down over time. "Choosing against the defaults," especially when those defaults tap into our desires for novelty, connection, or outrage, is fatiguing enough that eventually we give in.

"Giving in" is made easier by the fact that what we surrender to is so artfully designed. Tuned to our desires through sophisticated recommendation engines, our digital life is pleasant, addictive, endlessly binge-able.

Nietzsche is suspicious of anything that makes ease so . . . easy. The danger is not so much that ease will transform us into a race of weaklings; in fact, a world in which everyone had it easy might rid itself of much hate and war. No, the problem is that ease might succeed too well in the short term, producing a race of safe, secure, and comfortable people who are unwilling to risk their lives pushing forward the boundaries of humanity. In the long term, human greatness would be extinguished.

In his introduction to *The Gay Science*, Oxford professor Bernard Williams sums up Nietzsche's concern about "ease" soaking up the greatest quantity of our attention:

> The world might conceivably avoid destruction and overt hatred by organizing a pleasantly undemanding and unreflective way of life, a dazed but adequately efficient consumerism. Nietzsche probably did not think that such a society could survive in the long run, but in any case he could not reconcile himself to such a prospect or regard it as anything but loathsome. Contempt was one of his readier emotions, and nothing elicited it more than what he sometimes calls "the last man," the contented, unadventurous, philistine product of such a culture.

If we step back enough from the current technological paradigm to make sure our goals align with our considered values, we need not be nudged so easily by these external forces. We will be in a better position to use technology as a tool that serves our interests rather than its own.

All of which gets back to the core question: Are we actually equipped to sit back, think our lives through, and pluck a fulfilling set of life goals from the creative ether? Or are we so shaped by our context that we can't think beyond it?

The perennial search for meaning and happiness suggests that humans aren't so great at knowing what we most deeply desire. It's all well and good for Nietzsche to talk breezily about his joy-giving, self-overcoming, live-like-a-pirate life goals, but it's harder for us to come up with our own Yes and No. If it were clear and easy, more of us would already be living out our own straight lines.

Not for nothing was "know thyself" one of the inscriptions carved into the Temple of Apollo at Delphi. In one of his early *Untimely Meditations,* Nietzsche admits that this is a "hard saying" because Apollo is a god who "conceals nothing and says nothing, but only indicates." The responsibility for puzzling out the meaning of those hints falls ultimately upon us. "What does he indicate to you?" Nietzsche asks.

Still, Nietzsche thinks that we can gain some self-knowledge. He offers two main suggestions for doing so, which will provide the topics for our next two chapters. Both are at odds with the technical values of our day.

ONE: MANAGE INFORMATION FLOWS TO HEAR YOUR OWN VOICE.

This is a mental discipline, one focused explicitly on *restricting* words and ideas in healthy ways so that we do not gorge our minds to the detriment of our lives. One of Nietzsche's recurrent themes is how little we are capable of thinking for ourselves when our days are filled with the ideas and "voices" of others.

"How can anyone become a thinker if he does not spend at least a third of the day without passions, people, and books?" he asks in *Human, All Too Human*. In *Daybreak*, he identifies "the most general defect in our methods of education and training: nobody learns, nobody teaches, nobody wishes, to endure solitude."

Nietzsche wants space to reflect. It is not so much that, if we have enough peace and quiet, we can simply "think our way to meaningful goals" in some rational, Cartesian sense; it's more that solitude is a prerequisite for listening to our own lives. Only when we turn down the volume of the voices blaring and bleating at us can we also hear what our bodies, our passions, and our memories tell us.

This does not mean ceasing to read, listen, or connect. It does mean finding a way to accept and even to love the idea of *limits*. It means letting go of the anxiety that comes with having to know it all, to watch it all. It embraces informational fasting and forgetting, personal curation and rereading, disconnection and even the dreaded prospect of mental silence.

In that silence, as we soothe our restless distractibility, Nietzsche thinks we have a better-than-even chance of finding out what matters to us.

TWO: NURTURE A DEEP CONNECTION TO THE
EXTERNAL WORLD IN ORDER TO "REASON" WITH
YOUR BODY AND YOUR EMOTIONS.
This is a physical discipline, one focused on experiencing the world through our senses rather than our thoughts. We may try to reason our way toward meaningful lives—a useful exercise,

as discussed earlier—but Nietzsche argues that we *think through the body as well.*

"Behind your thoughts and feelings," says Zarathustra, "stands a powerful commander, an unknown wise man—he is called self. He lives in your body, he is your body. There is more reason in your body than in your best wisdom."

Nietzsche makes this point when drawing on his Lutheran heritage with a pithy remark about *faith* and *works.* This was one of the great Protestant issues, going back to Martin Luther. The dominant position was that *faith* was primary; only out of this trust in God flowed a person's "good works" as a response to God's goodness and grace.

But Nietzsche thinks that this gets human psychology exactly wrong.

"I say, let us first and foremost have works!" he bellows. "And this means practice! Practice! Practice! The necessary faith will come later—be certain of that." Action in the world helps condition what and how we believe. We aren't going to sit around *thinking* our way to enlightenment or to happiness.

The "powerful commander" of the body itself, working in and even against the world through exercise or art or skilled craftsmanship, offers a lesson in what matters. We ignore the pleasure of our muscles and our senses at our peril. Nietzsche thus advocates an experimental approach; engage in action and let the body itself speak to you about what it needs.

THESE APPROACHES TO self-knowledge shed light on our truest needs and deepest motivations. In periods of mental silence, those deep needs may become clearer, and we may find that they differ from the ones offered by our technological paradigm.

We simply cannot know, in advance of such reflection, how best to deploy our digital tools (or if we need them at all). Tips or "hacks" have little to offer us. Negative prescriptions fail to move us. But as we develop a positive creative vision, we can start to sense if our tech habits help or harm it, and we can reform practices that do not serve us well. Here's how McGinn lays out the vision:

> Inspired by the Nietzschean ideal of human excellence, the individual either would avoid traffic with technologies likely to engender in him inertial or dissipative behavior, e.g., the technology of the assembly line or technologies designed to make life "frictionless," or, put positively, would use a particular technology only to the extent that he possessed the power of discrimination and it possessed the characteristics enabling him to turn it—directly or indirectly—to life-affirming and life-enhancing ends and effects.

In his response to suffering and alienation, in his focus on *living* as opposed to *thinking*, and in his refusal to let human creativity be trampled by the machine, Nietzsche remains electrifying despite his short circuits. In a world now dominated by technologies of ease, he reminds us of the limits of frictionless digital hedonism—and of the merits of having a Yes, a No, a straight line, a *goal*.

Three

THE INFORMATION DIET

Asceticism and Attention

IN HIS YOUTH, BEFORE HE BECAME THE MOST FAMOUS preacher in Constantinople, John Chrysostom was a Syrian monk. He retreated from urban life in Antioch during the 370s CE and found his way out to caves in the mountains outside town. There he joined a group of ascetics who wore animal skins and ate a single meal each day—bread and salt. (The luxury-minded among them might add a bit of oil; the sick and the weak would also get green vegetables and lentils.)

This regimen proved insufficiently strict, and John retreated for 2 years to an even more distant cave where he could live completely alone, pray, and avoid most bodily pleasures, including sleep. According to his biographer Palladius, John never lay completely flat; if he did eventually give in to exhaustion, he slept sitting down or leaning against the rocky wall. By the end of the second year, he felt worn out and ill; Palladius says that his "gastric regions were deadened, and the functions of his kidneys were impaired by the intense cold." He returned to Antioch and became a priest.

In the desert, John drew a bounding horizon around much of human experience so that he could focus on those few things that he felt truly mattered in life. His embrace of extreme limits is seen across religious traditions, in both strict and quite loose forms, suggesting that humanity has some deep-seated need for ascetic renunciation.

Nietzsche is well known for his hatred of asceticism. He saw it as turning one's back on life, a No-saying to the world. "The ascetic treats life as a wrong road on which one must finally walk back to the point where it begins," he complains, "or as a mistake that is put right by deeds."

Nietzsche's basic project is to affirm life, even in its most difficult and painful aspects. He says that he does not even "want to wage war against ugliness."

> I do not want to accuse, I do not want even to accuse the accusers. Looking aside—let that be my sole negation! . . . I wish to be at any time hereafter only a yes-sayer!

Yet even Nietzsche the Yes-sayer came to admit the value— no, the *necessity*—of the ascetic attitude.

Life itself is a given thing, and it exists within certain brute barriers, such as the reality of death and the need to "waste" much of our lives in sleep. Ignoring those limits guarantees unhappiness; we can only flourish by accepting them. Then there are limits that are not imposed upon us by biology but which are freely chosen in order to thrive—limits to sexual activity, to eating and drinking, to playing video games 8 hours a day.

Nietzsche supported such limits. This may sound strange coming from the champion of the self-overcoming *übermensch,* but he acknowledges the reality and necessity of them even in his earliest work.

And this is a universal law: a living thing can be healthy, strong, and fruitful only when bounded by a horizon.

This sense of the value of limits allows the banished ascetic spirit to slip in through the back door. Though Nietzsche opposes attempts to bypass or denigrate the body and its senses, he also recognizes a need for boundaries around our experiences. That's because, as finite creatures, an infinite Yes-saying—whether to food, to books, or to relationships—would hobble us. We simply lack the time to indulge every life option; even if we proved immortal, many of the options on offer would prove toxic. The wrong text message, read at the wrong time, can be a killer.

Nietzsche flips asceticism on its head. He accepts the need for restriction, for discipline, for No-saying, but only when it is done in the service of life. That is why we find Nietzsche late in his career saying things such as, "All honor to the ascetic ideal *insofar as it is honest*! so long as it believes in itself and does not play tricks on us!"

Asceticism might seem like a strange departure gate for a journey into "information and its discontents." It sounds alien and harsh, a world of hair shirts and pole-sitting that has little to offer the modern age. But, in our world of abundance, we may need to rediscover the idea. Our digital ecosystem has created, collected, and curated so much content that even to sample its riches feels hopeless, like a skinny kid confronted with the world's largest Greek *meze* platter. And, though some of this information sits silently on data center servers and library shelves awaiting our interest, much more has been weaponized to seek us out, to proactively appeal, to cram us well beyond satiety.

Andrew Sullivan, the controversial polemicist and an early convert to blogging, focused most of his work on politics. Yet even when bounded within this domain, the amount of information he faced became incapacitating. In a 2016 essay, Sullivan wrote about how constant reading and writing had made him feel spiritually and mentally and physically adrift:

> I tried reading books, but that skill now began to elude me. After a couple of pages, my fingers twitched for a keyboard. I tried meditation, but my mind bucked and bridled as I tried to still it. I got a steady workout routine, and it gave me the only relief I could measure for an hour or so a day. But over time in this pervasive virtual world, the online clamor grew louder and louder. Although I spent hours each day, alone and silent, attached to a laptop, it felt as if I were in a constant cacophonous crowd of words and images, sounds and ideas, emotions and tirades—a wind tunnel of deafening, deadening noise. So much of it was irresistible, as I fully understood. So much of the technology was irreversible, as I also knew. But I'd begun to fear that this new way of living was actually becoming a way of not-living.

We do not have to like it, but many of our longings and responses are evolutionarily fitted to a pre-technological world. We reflect that world and its patterns in complex ways. If we disrupt them too thoroughly, too quickly, there are consequences.

We saw earlier that technology critic Neil Postman calls the modern flood of information "a form of garbage, not only incapable of answering the most fundamental human questions but barely useful in providing coherent direction to the solution of even mundane problems." Such garbage does not simply smell bad. Without coherence, informational garbage can actually harm us "when it has no place to go, when there is no theory to which it applies, no pattern in which it fits, when there is no higher purpose that it serves." This is disorienting, and it engenders feelings of chaos and confusion.

Avoiding informational garbage requires us to make sometimes painful choices about what (and how much) we read, listen to, and watch. But many of us have lost the communities and traditions that in past centuries helped to shape and even constrain our life choices; instead, we have embraced a boundless global freedom. This can be liberating, but we also risk incoherence or simply wasting our time. In the absence of tradition or culture or religion or some other organizing principle, commerce can easily sway our choices. Matthew Crawford, in *The World Beyond Your Head*, sees the problem this way:

> As autonomous individuals, we often find ourselves isolated in a fog of choices. Our mental lives become shapeless, and more susceptible to whatever presents itself out of the ether. But of course these presentations are highly orchestrated; commercial forces step into the void of cultural authority.

Our attention is the searchlight that can cut through the fog of choices, showing a coherent path forward. The problem is that our attention is unavoidably limited. We *must* choose how to spend it if we want to spend it in any coherent way. "To attend to anything in a sustained way requires actively excluding all the other things that grab at our attention," Crawford says. "It requires, if not ruthlessness toward oneself, a capacity for self-regulation."

Ruthlessness toward oneself—we are not so far from Chrysostom here, are we?

This need to discipline our attention is well captured in Alan Jacobs's 2016 piece "Attending to Technology: Theses for Disputation." His first two points:

1. Everything begins with attention.
2. The question of what I should give attention to is inseparable from the question of what I should decline to give attention to.

"Attention given to one thing cannot be given, then and there, to another," Jacobs adds. "And no moment comes to us twice."

I have been far too prodigal with my own attention, an occupational hazard for those who live "online." For the past 15 years, I worked in front of a screen through which I monitored my world like a spider waiting motionless in the center of a web. Every delicate tremor—an email, a Twitter notification, a breaking news link pasted into our corporate chat room—would send me scuttling off in search of the next morsel to fill some kind of yawning info-chasm within.

Some of this was essential to my work as a journalist. The information I acquired often led to stories that (hopefully) educated and (perhaps) entertained the reading public. But let's be honest: much of it did not. Working constantly at a computer where distraction was never more than a click away, I became that guy who knew a bit about everything from Alaskan oil to Zambian cuisine—so long as it had been covered in the *New York Times*, the *Washington Post*, the *Guardian*, or a dozen other papers that week. I had Deep Thoughts on everything from health-care policy to intellectual property—so long as they had been covered in *Atlantic* or *New Yorker* think pieces. I was awash in memes and other "viral" content shared by colleagues and friends. Much of this information was acquired for no real purpose; little of it affected my life.

More disturbing were my new habits of mind. Like some kind of laboratory animal, I responded instantly to stimuli such as the arrival of a new email, a chat notification, a text on my phone. The reward for this response was some tiny fragment of novelty, something that might be more interesting or important—though it usually wasn't—than what I was currently doing. It was a 15-year-long education in training my attention to flick rather than to focus. My thoughts too often felt jumpy and jumbled.

By not discriminating about what I most needed, about what truly mattered, about where I wanted to spend my attention, I blew tens of thousands of hours digesting material that was ultimately of limited value to my life. As Postman notes, every educational institution must manage information to teach what its students need to learn. It will do this, "to a large extent, by excluding information." This is as true in the school of life as anywhere else.

Let's put this in perspective. Counting *only* the hundreds of hours I spent reading horse-race coverage of the 2016 and 2020 US presidential elections, I could have learned to play some of my favorite Chopin nocturnes. These are hard pieces for a wretched pianist like myself, but mastering their difficulty would have been infinitely more satisfying than reading anything about Donald Trump.

We are shaped by that to which we attend. The shaping process exerted on our minds by smartphones and constant Internet usage often involves interruption, skimming, aimless clicking, and a constant desire for novelty. This is not *all* that it involves, but years of online immersion gave me more of these things than I had hoped. They are not the habits of mind I want to develop—and it has taken more years to start shaking free of them.

There's no point in getting too rigorous or regretful about such things; humans have been ingenious time wasters for millennia. But when so many people report real distress over the amount and quality of the time spent with their digital tools, we might wonder if we can do better. To navigate our Information Age, we need to control the attention we pay to "content"—even the term treats information as a commodity—which means learning how to tune out.

Nietzsche's own illness, which forced him away from the books he used to love, made him unusually sensitive to the ways that information consumption affects a life. As such, he is a surprisingly useful guide on our ascetic journey.

Information as Nutrition

You don't have to read much philosophy to know that it tends to emphasize words, distinctions, and ideas over biological needs—like dinner. What has an egg roll to do with speech act theory?

Yet Nietzsche valued nutrition. Because he saw humans not as brains trapped in bodies but as creatures of the earth—creatures driven by basic biology more than most professional thinkers, then or now, like to admit—eating and drinking mattered. In his autobiography, *Ecce Homo*, he devotes several pages to discussing what he drinks. (Water, no alcohol, though he could apparently pack away the booze when a young man.) Even with a breakdown weeks away, Nietzsche recognized that this was not standard philosophical practice, so he explains why he writes this way:

> I shall be asked why I have really narrated all these little things which according to the traditional judgement are matters of indifference. . . . Answer: these little things— nutriment, place, climate, recreation, the whole casu- istry of selfishness—are beyond all conception of greater importance than anything that has been considered of importance hitherto. It is precisely here that one has to begin to learn anew.

Elsewhere in the book, he puts the matter even more pro- vocatively, saying, "I am much more interested in a question on which the 'salvation of humanity' depends far more than on any theologians' curio: the question of *nutrition*."

Though serious about his own diet, Nietzsche also uses nutri- tion as a metaphor. It stands for every human process of ongoing replenishment, processing, and elimination. As with food, too little information can kill us, while too much makes us ill.

Nietzsche felt this illness during his professorship at Basel. He burned up his energy and imagination there, he says in *Ecce Homo*, without taking proper measures to replenish them. Note the language of food:

> During my Basel period my whole spiritual diet, includ- ing the way I divided up my day, was a completely sense- less abuse of extraordinary resources, without any new supply to cover this consumption in any way, without even any thought about consumption and replenishment.

He had written this way for some time. In *On the Genealogy of Morals*, Nietzsche compares experience in general with the act of eating. "A strong and well-constituted man digests his experiences (his deeds and misdeeds included) as he digests his meals," he says, "even when he has to swallow some tough morsels." Remember how Nietzsche describes his Basel experience:

> I moved out of the house of the scholars, and I even slammed the door behind me. Too long did my soul sit hungry at their table; I am not, as they are, trained to pursue understanding as a kind of nut-cracking. . . . I am too hot and burned by my own thoughts: often it almost takes my breath away . . . but they sit coolly in the cool shade: they want in all things to be mere spectators and are wary of sitting where the sun burns down upon the steps.

Nietzsche's essential loneliness and hunger radiate from the page like the heat of the sun-scorched steps that he describes. If you have ever felt burnout as a knowledge worker or have ever worked in the academy, perhaps the frustration on display resonates. Nietzsche was, from his earliest writings, committed to academic study not as an "idler in the garden of knowledge," not as someone who could "turn comfortably away from life and action," but only insofar as it "serves life." He could never reconcile himself to a community of scholars who did not see things the same way.

When he left the university behind, Nietzsche also abandoned its "know everything" ethos. He loved ideas, but he reacted strongly to the prospect of information crowding out one's own reflections. He wrote increasingly about the value of selective rather than comprehensive reading, the need to read slowly and then to reread (and thus cover less material), and the importance of forgetting.

His approach to information was bound up with his goal-driven approach to life. Anyone focused on constant novelty and omnivorous consumption will not have either the time, the self-direction, or the mental clarity to pursue creative excellence. Nietzsche came to value instead his own thoughts and his own voice, which he worked to develop by freeing time for them.

Nietzsche's rants about "herd mentality" don't feel counter-cultural today, in our individualist world. But his approach to information still feels rebellious. It requires us to make peace with certain kinds of personal ignorance. It demands that we limit the constant interruptions of texts, emails, social media feeds, and phone calls. It celebrates depth over breadth, focused consideration over skimming. It deprecates the value of novelty.

Taken together, Nietzsche's approach to information might make it harder to gab around the water cooler about what happened on this season of *Stranger Things*. It might become more difficult to offer pithy cocktail party comments, gleaned from a zealous reading of the *New York Times*, about French cheese-making in the Loire valley. But Nietzsche's information diet might also improve our mental health.

Slow Content

No one ever accused Nietzsche of modesty. The man was con-vinced of his own world-shaking destiny, which must have been tough to sustain when only a few hundred people were reading his books. Still, Nietzsche offered his then-nonexistent reader-ship tips for properly absorbing his works—especially his more "aphoristic" books. Nietzsche describes his ideal reader in the preface to *Daybreak*:

> A book like this, a problem like this, is in no hurry; we both, I just as much of my book, are friends of *lento* [slowness]. It is not for nothing that I have been a philologist, perhaps I am a philologist still, that is to say, a teacher of slow reading:—in the end I also write slowly. Nowadays it is not only my habit, it is also to my taste—a malicious taste, perhaps?—no longer to write anything which does not reduce to despair every sort of man who is "in a hurry."

Anyone who has tried to read *Daybreak* straight through, as though it were a novel, will run headlong into Nietzsche's "malicious taste." The goal was to craft a form that embodies the qualities encouraged by the content: pithy nuggets demanding careful thought, mental experimentation, and wide-ranging curiosity about morality and psychology. By *forcing* his readers to proceed slowly if they want to make sense of the book, Nietzsche puts a preemptive stop to bingeing.

This call to read more slowly, and with greater engagement, is not reserved for Nietzsche's books. In the same preface, he speaks more widely about European culture, which he thought valued speed and productivity above all else. (Sound familiar?) But we must value the ability to "go aside, to take time, to become still, to become slow," because careful thinking is "delicate, cautious work" that "achieves nothing if it does not achieve it *lento*."

Do we *want* to process information this way? Nietzsche thinks we do—that we will be enchanted by the opportunity to go slow in an "age of 'work': that is to say, of haste, of unseemly and immoderate hurry-skurry." We must learn instead to "read well: i.e. slowly, profoundly, attentively, prudently, with inner thoughts, with the mental doors ajar, with delicate fingers and eyes."

To consume information slowly becomes, in this telling, an act of resistance against a dehumanizing technological order. Much like the Slow Food movement, Nietzsche's Slow Content assumes a political and ethical dimension. When it comes to our information diet, it matters *how* we read, watch, and listen.

It's not clear that many people today believe this, though. If "slow reading" is so liberating, why has every lit major with a Twitter feed written a thread about how they once loved big Russian novels such as *Anna Karenina* but now struggle to make it through lifestyle articles in the newspaper? In one sense, the reasons are obvious. We have too many tabs open! Someone texts me after each paragraph I read! I'm watching Netflix on my second monitor right now!

And yet, given the discomfort so many people express about binge-driven, skim-oriented, hyperlinked culture, one might expect more cultural support for slow reading. There is some— apps that store long articles for later reading, the whole genre of "longreads," the continued existence of the *New Yorker*. But it's hard to fight those dopamine hits of novelty that make sustained attention so difficult.

This can be true even in the centers of learning. English professor Mark Bauerlein complains, in the course of commenting on the Nietzsche passages above, that universities also struggle with slow reading.

Young people today process more words than ever before and in faster time—*allegro*, not *lento*. To meet them, more classrooms and more course assignments follow suit, for instance, assigning blogs instead of papers, short readings instead of long ones. The unfortunate truth is that fast reading and fast writing don't make people more flexible, more capable of slow reading and writing when the situation demands them.

The faster information can move, the more we love it. But speed itself can have costs. As Henry David Thoreau remarked about the technology of his time, "We are in great haste to construct a magnetic telegraph from Maine to Texas; but Maine and Texas, it may be, have nothing important to communicate. . . . As if the main object were to talk fast and not to talk sensibly." He worried that "our inventions are wont to be pretty toys, which distract our attention from serious things. They are but improved means to an unimproved end."

Nietzsche calls us to consciously resist speed and to guard our attention and deploy it in focused ways. Just as jamming food into one's belly is liable to feel bad, information too should be consumed at a certain pace and with a certain care. As with food, there are always exceptions—the quick snack on the run, the rushed meal before the concert—but they are the exceptions that prove the rule.

Ruminants

Becoming one of the "friends of *lento*" sounds great—like joining an exclusive club. You, at least, will not become one of those degenerates who text their way through dinner parties and who have given up on novels! But there are implications to the Nietzsche Diet, some less convenient than others. Much as Slow Food demands good ingredients, Slow Content demands a certain quality of material.

Amid climate change, global pandemics, and a rising wave of authoritarianism, we might desire nothing but a dumb comedy at the end of the week. Or we might seek cathartic release in online outrage. Or we might obsessively consume the news. We may want, that is, the information equivalent of fast food. No matter how good it may feel, though, we need to limit this kind of content consumption to keep ourselves healthy.

Nietzsche was convinced that human life is about transformation and transcendence, and that our best hope for achieving them is reflection in the presence of strong ideas. That is, much of our reading and listening and watching should focus on artists and thinkers and friends who have something meaningful to say.

Arthur Schopenhauer, to whose philosophy Nietzsche was devoted as a young man, once wrote, "The art of not reading is a very important one." Schopenhauer assumed most popular books were rubbish on the grounds that "he who writes for fools always finds a large public." And so, for him, "a precondition for reading good books is not reading bad ones: for life is short."

Nietzsche embraces this idea of "not reading" and turns it into a radical principle of selection. He praises people who have an instinctive sense for the material that will matter to their lives. "What is it, fundamentally, that allows us to recognize *who has turned out well*?" Nietzsche asks.

What does not kill him makes him stronger. Instinctively, he collects from everything he sees, hears, lives through, *his* sum: he is a principle of selection, he discards much. He is always in his own company, whether

he associates with books, human beings, or landscapes:
he honors by *choosing*, by *admitting*, by *trusting*.

Such people do not indiscriminately welcome content into
their world. They are "principles of selection," thoughtful about
what they choose to admit, because each admission is an act of
trust. If we are going to put ourselves in the hands of a writer
or a director or even a conversation partner, and if we are going
to give that person our full attention over the course of many
hours, we hope that the process will be worthwhile. We are
shaped by what we consume, which makes our information
inputs not just matters of aesthetic taste but also matters of morals and ethics.

Few are worthy of such trust. In his early career, Nietzsche
names only eight: Epicurus, Montaigne, Goethe, Spinoza, Plato,
Rousseau, Pascal, and Schopenhauer. Only from them, he says,
"will I accept judgment." He has judged them important enough
that they will guide all his habits of mind. "In all that I say, conclude, or think out for myself and others, I fasten my eyes on
those eight and see their eyes fastened on mine," he writes.

You may not be surprised to learn that Nietzsche is exag-
gerating. He read widely in areas such as evolutionary theory,
science, and moral philosophy, and his letters contain numerous
requests for books and other materials. (He of course had to read
widely to find his "personal eight" in the first place.) But he was
completely serious about the importance of selection and restriction; this was how he could, in the end, get by with only that
single trunk of books.

In a world that was even then inundated with more information than one human could possibly manage, Nietzsche calls
for a revolution in attitude. It is not about a proud illiteracy or

a refusal to read widely; it is simply a recognition that humans have limited time for both thought and action. To spend so much of that time consuming novel or "news-y" content of ancillary value to our lives seems to Nietzsche a waste.

The further implication of the Nietzsche Diet is that we will digest our Slow Content like ruminants chewing the cud. As we identify the information that matters deeply to our lives, we will return to it many times. "One thing is necessary above all if one is to practice reading as an art in this way, something that has been unlearned most thoroughly nowadays," writes Nietzsche in *On the Genealogy of Morals*. "Something for which one has almost to be a cow and in any case not a 'modern man': rumination."

He is not talking about "great works" that we experience once so that we can pass a test or sprinkle cultural references throughout our letters to the editor. What Nietzsche holds up for "rumination" are the movies we could watch a hundred times, the books we have dog-eared into submission, the music that might rewire our brains. To these things we give our trust, and they reward it.

In *Ecce Homo*, Nietzsche makes this point clearly:

> I almost always seek refuge with the same books—actually, a small number—books *proved to me*. Perhaps it is not my way to read much, or diverse things: a reading room makes me sick. Nor is it my way to love much, or diverse things. Caution, even hostility against new books comes closer to my instincts.

This was not a new sentiment. One hundred years earlier the English essayist William Hazlitt wrote, "I hate to read new books. There are twenty or thirty volumes that I have read over and over again, and these are the only ones that I have any desire ever to read at all. . . . The dust and smoke and noise of modern literature have nothing in common with the pure, silent air of immortality."

The Nietzsche Diet features a crucial trade-off: Slow and repeated reading of your personal canon can transform your life, but you will necessarily be deeper than you are broad. Nietzsche is . . . okay with this. "Once and for all," he writes, "there is a great deal I do not want to know.—Wisdom sets bounds even to knowledge."

This approach can be extreme; for instance, if you literally read just eight authors, I might ask whether you are open enough to the stunning diversity of the world. But as a general principle that we should more carefully curate our information intake, Nietzsche's approach offers a counterweight to a world in which indiscriminate information has become the intellectual equivalent of "empty calories."

Nietzsche gives us the courage to resist the tyranny of the new, and he provides the space for us to master (or to be mastered by) the works we consume. This pursuit of mastery—insofar as we *are* capable of choosing our personal canons well—is far more likely to end in personal transformation than is any unfocused, onetime consumption of trivial information.

But can we choose our personal canons well? And how are we to do so if we don't read widely enough to know what's out there? Nietzsche offers little practical guidance, talking instead in big-picture advice. "What am I really doing, and what do I mean by doing it?" he suggests that we ask ourselves. "That is the question of truth which is not taught under our present system of education, and consequently not asked, because there is no time for it."

So committed is Nietzsche to the idea that we each have our own path—even our own morality—that he offers little beyond the Delphic Oracle's injunction to "know thyself" and some complaints about how few of us do.

Perhaps our course of life offers clarity. Youth and early adulthood lend themselves naturally to wide exploration; I think we would all suspect that anyone who closed a "personal canon" at 17 lacks the basis for doing this well. But as we age, we come to know both ourselves and the world better. At some point, we may want to be shaped by certain writers or directors or musicians.

I experienced this as I entered my forties. The wide reading in philosophy, literature, and technology that characterized my early years gradually lost some of its interest. I found myself, though still hungry for the new, increasingly attuned to the old—material that can be mined again for pleasure and profit, material that can shape me. I will miss out on some new discoveries, but the march of years makes this less concerning. Given how little of even the *best* content I will consume in my life, there seems little sense in trying to master everything. Instead I find my own principles of selection narrowing as Nietzsche describes them. Increasingly, I want works "proved to me" by time. And on each reading, viewing, or listening, I judge anew—in the face of always-increasing life experience—whether this is a work that should "remain in the collection."

This sounds incredibly serious—all peas and no French fries. But it need not be. One of the heroes of my personal pantheon, in works that have been tested by 20-plus years of rereading, is the British comic genius P.G. Wodehouse. His Jeeves and Wooster novels are sublimely ludicrous farces of no particular heft, yet I would lose all my philosophy before losing Wodehouse. He was of course a master of his craft, an expert plotter and a true lover of words. But his view of the world is one I need: a place wondrous even amid danger, where laughter can bring down dictators and aunts alike, where joy *does* come in the morning. It is a profoundly comic view of life. And it is no less "serious" about that for not being, well, serious. Wodehouse rewards my repeated attention.

Even if you value novelty far more than Nietzsche, perhaps you can take something from his somewhat curmudgeonly commentary: Approach information with your eyes open. With every texting relationship, every group chat, every email chain, every book we read, every series we binge, every link we click— we place our fragile attention in the hands of someone else. It is an act of trust, and we benefit from taking that act seriously.

Info Dump

Unleash the jokes—it's time to move our metaphor down the alimentary canal. We have discussed what information we consume and how we consume it, but Nietzsche's unique take may be most apparent in his praise of *information evacuation*. That is—forgetting.

"Forgetting is essential to action of any kind, just as not only light but darkness too is essential for the life of everything organic," he writes in an early essay. "It is possible to live almost without memory, and to live happily moreover, as the animal demonstrates; but it is altogether impossible to *live* at all without forgetting."

Our brains are notoriously selective. They latch onto the new and they remember the extraordinary, but unchanging stimuli are quickly filtered and forgotten. This can be frustrating, but discarding information seems necessary in order to focus our attention and to take action. Indiscriminate processing and retention of *all* incoming stimuli would truly turn information into garbage; we would be swamped.

This is essentially the plot of the Jorge Luis Borges short story "Funes, His Memory" from the 1944 collection *Artifices*. In the piece, the narrator encounters one Ireneo Funes, a young man from a poor part of Argentina. His "gift" is a perfect memory, but this turns out to be a paralyzing curse. The narrator explains why:

> With one quick look, you and I perceive three wine-glasses on a table; Funes perceived every grape that had been pressed into the wine and all the stalks and tendrils of its vineyard. He knew the forms of the clouds in the southern sky on the morning of April 30, 1882, and he could compare them in his memory with the veins in the marbled binding of a book he had seen only once, or with the feathers of spray lifted by an oar on the Río Negro on the eve of the Battle of Quebracho. Nor were those memories simple—every visual image was linked to muscular sensations, thermal sensations, and so on. He was able to reconstruct every dream, every daydream he had ever had. Two or three times he had reconstructed an entire day; he had never erred or faltered, but each reconstruction had itself taken an entire day.

The story concludes with the observation that "to think is to ignore (or forget) differences, to generalize, to abstract. In the teeming world of Ireneo Funes there was nothing but particulars—and they were virtually immediate particulars."

Borges's story is not mere fiction. We know that certain human minds can maintain a nearly photographic memory— but we also know that this can be disruptive. Jill Price, a 42-year-old United Kingdom woman said to have "hyperthymestic syndrome," in 2008 described the experience of being able to recall every day of her life since she was 14.

"Some memories are good and give me a warm, safe feeling," she told the *Telegraph* newspaper. "But I also recall every bad decision, insult and excruciating embarrassment. Over the years it has eaten me up. It has kind of paralysed me. . . . My memory is too strong. It's like a running movie that never stops. Most have called it a gift. But I call it a burden. I run my entire life through my head every day and it drives me crazy!"

We must be able to rid ourselves of what does not serve us. Nietzsche sees this as more than a passive process; it is an active bit of mental meal prep, as we decide which bits of information we will literally "in-corporate" within our body as memories. Consider this long passage linking nutrition and forgetfulness from *On the Genealogy of Morals*:

> Forgetfulness is . . . an active—in the strictest sense, positive—inhibiting capacity, responsible for the fact that what we absorb through experience impinges as little on our consciousness during its digestion (what might be called its "psychic assimilation") as does the whole manifold process of our physical nourishment, that of so-called "physical assimilation."
>
> The temporary shutting of the doors and windows of consciousness; guaranteed freedom from disturbance by the noise and struggle caused by our underworld of

obedient organs as they co-operate with and compete against one another; a little silence, a little *tabula rasa* of consciousness, making room for the new, making room above all for the superior functions and functionaries—those of governing, anticipating, planning ahead (since our organism is structured as an oligarchy)—such is the use of what I have called active forgetfulness, an active forgetfulness whose function resembles that of a concierge preserving mental order, calm, and decorum. On this basis one may appreciate immediately to what extent there could be no happiness, no serenity, no hope, no pride, no *present* without forgetfulness.

On the other hand, Nietzsche says, the scientific worldview "hates forgetting, which is the death of knowledge, and seeks to abolish all limitations of horizon and launch mankind upon an infinite and unbounded sea of light whose light is knowledge of all becoming."

This is an apt description of our technological approach to information. From Google to the NSA, the motto is: *Collect it all; keep it all.* If you run up against storage limits, build another data center. But this strategy won't work for individual minds. Accepting our inclination to forget is to accept our human finitude. To hate forgetting is to lash out against limits; it is an attack on the necessity of selection and curation.

Years ago, I enrolled in an English literature PhD program and spent two happy and then two more less-happy years reading everything I could find about the English Renaissance. By the end of it, I could trace the Book of Common Prayer's key revisions or tell you which of the "Caroline divines" had the ear of King Charles at any given moment. I had read every play by Ben Jonson and every word of *The Faerie Queene*. I forced my way through more terrible sixteenth-century poetry than one person should ever have to read.

Set aside for a moment the question of why it felt important to know these things. The point is that I did want to know them and spent an enormous amount of time consuming the 400-year-old literature and history of a small island. Yet when I decided to pursue a career as a writer instead of a literature professor, I was shocked at how quickly this knowledge fell away. Two years on, sitting at the dinner table or in the library, I would realize suddenly that I could no longer say anything about the Earl of Essex or the third act of *The Two Gentlemen of Verona*. Nor could I remember if the Solemn League and Covenant was pro- or anti-Presbyterian. Or was it unrelated to Presbyterianism at all? Later I struggled to remember the dates of each English king and queen. Panic set in over losing so quickly what had cost so much to learn. What was the point of any intellectual endeavor if our minds were so apt to let us down?

But I eventually realized three things. First, I *could* have retained that information. I simply had to stay in the academy, toiling through seminars focused on the daily work of the Westminster Assembly and writing papers on the Inkhorn Controversy. It was my choice to disengage finally from that world; forgetting was a natural consequence. My body was releasing information that I had told it, through my actions, was no longer essential to life.

Second, I had lost many details but retained the results. Attitudes toward history and scholarship, habits of mind, patterns of critical reading, each had shaped me, and I remained in the new shape they imposed. The acquisition of knowledge changed the way I thought, even if some of the underlying data dissipated into the mists of the mind.

Finally, I saw that forgetfulness might serve as a hedge against anxiety. Because there *is* an anxiety attending information consumption in a limitless world. When have I read and watched and listened to enough? Another best-selling book, another prestige TV drama, another true-crime podcast—there's always more. But in time I took comfort from the fact that soon I would forget so much of it. And if that were true, then it was not necessary that I "keep up," that I try to consume it all. I could instead accept information with gratitude, focus on maintaining whatever personal canon I judged important to my life, and relax about the rest.

Nietzsche wants us to welcome this process of forgetting. Attempts to hold on to the past can prevent us from entering the present, and it is in that Dionysian embrace of present existence that we experience happiness.

> It is always the same thing that makes happiness happiness: the ability to forget. . . . He who cannot sink down on the threshold of the moment and forget all the past, who cannot stand balanced like a goddess of victory without growing dizzy and afraid, will never know what happiness is—worse, he will never do anything to make others happy.

Forgetting—the beginning of morals?

It's a simple message: When it comes to information, do not be afraid. Open your hands and let information pass through them like sand. What remains after the sifting may not be perfect, but it will be enough.

Fasting

The final part of the Nietzsche Diet is a practice that every good ascetic must master: fasting.

It is not enough to become a disciplined information curator immersing oneself repeatedly in the finest sources of knowledge and entertainment. It is not enough to adopt the ways of Slow Content or to forget aggressively. Sometimes we must forgo information altogether.

Consider Nietzsche's complaint in *Daybreak* about people who are constantly distracted by each day's news: "Whatever may be your desire to accomplish great deeds, the deep silence of pregnancy never comes to you!" Nietzsche says about such lives. "The event of the day sweeps you along like straws before the wind."

This describes many of my days in journalism, where chasing the "event of the day" is part of the job. Many of us would benefit from more of the "deep silence of pregnancy," where thought grows and develops until it is truly ready to be born. We need more silence and more solitude.

How much of this info-fasting do we need? We have already seen Nietzsche's tongue-in-cheek answer: "How can anyone become a thinker if he does not spend at least a third of the day without passions, people, and books?"

Nietzsche sometimes claims that we need even more separation. In fact, when writing something long, Nietzsche avoided both people and other books completely. "At times when I am deeply sunk in work you will see no books around me," he says. "I would guard against letting anyone speak or even think in my vicinity. And that is what reading would mean."

As we've seen, Nietzsche famously found creative solitude in long walks. He would ramble for hours at a time in the paths around the alpine town of Sils Maria, Switzerland, where he often spent his post-Basel summers. No books, no companions—just Friedrich and a collection of small journals where he could jot down thoughts as he hiked.

"To set to early in the morning, at the break of day, in all the fulness and dawn of one's strength, and to read a book—this I call positively vicious!" he says.

His concern, here as everywhere, is that what makes us unique is too easily drowned out by a background drone of information. In the end, Nietzsche worries that we will know only how to react to someone else's creation and not how to find our own creative voice. He is especially hard on the profession he left behind, writing:

> The scholar who, in truth, does little else than handle books—with the philologist of average attainments their number may amount to two hundred a day—ultimately forgets entirely and completely the capacity of thinking for himself. When he has not a book between his fingers he cannot think. When he thinks, he responds to a stimulus (a thought he has read)—finally all he does is to react.

While modern digital technology encourages a kind of solitude—just me and my screen!—it is not generally a ruminative, pregnant solitude.

This is a persistent theme of technology critics. "Smartphones are the primary enabler of solitude deprivation," says Cal Newport. "Technology gives us more and more of what we think we want," writes Sherry Turkle, "but if we pay attention to the real consequences of what we think we want, we may discover what we really want. We may want some stillness and solitude."

Nietzsche agrees—though as usual, he is far more quotable. "Noise murders thought," he says.

All this talk about fasting from information presumes two things. First, that we *want* to be alone with our thoughts. For many of us, constant information has become mental junk food that we consume precisely to avoid our own mind and its anxieties. Second, that we have the mental resources to make solitude productive rather than boring.

Nietzsche, looking around at his own society, worried that the will to speed and to novelty was creating a class of people who had no peace within themselves. They wanted only to escape their thoughts and give themselves to every momentary distraction. But even if they could cultivate solitude, they lacked the creative and intellectual resources to do anything useful with it.

> All of you for whom furious labor is dear and what is fast,
> and new, and strange—you tolerate yourselves poorly,
> your industry is flight and the will to forget yourselves.
> If you believed in life more, you would throw yourselves
> away less in the moment. But for waiting you lack suf-
> ficient capacity—and even for laziness!

While most of the Nietzsche Diet has focused on selection, on restriction, on fasting, these are techniques to *profit* from a world gorging itself on information. They are not an admonition to renounce information itself.

In the end, we should return refreshed to the broader world.

"Why this solitude?" a voice asks in one of Nietzsche's aphorisms. "I am not angry with anybody," Nietzsche replies, "but when I am alone it seems to me that I can see my friends in a clearer and rosier light than when I am with them. And when I loved and felt music best I lived far from it. It would seem that I must have distant perspectives in order that I may think well of things."

As Nietzsche critic Robert Miner sums up Nietzsche's thought here, "Contact with friends and books is good. Yet a healthy relation to either is impossible unless one has a substantial freedom from both."

The Meal

Tony Fadell is one of the original inventors of both the iPod and the iPhone. In 2018, the former Apple engineer wrote an op-ed in *Wired* about unhealthy device usage, a piece in which he went all-in on the "information as food" metaphor. Fadell didn't argue to restrict device usage to some "healthy level," however; he argued that we don't even know what a healthy level is—and that it might vary by person.

> Take healthy eating as an analogy: we have advice from scientists and nutritionists on how much protein and carbohydrate we should include in our diet; we have standardised scales to measure our weight against; and we have norms for how much we should exercise.
>
> But when it comes to digital "nourishment," we don't know what a "vegetable," a "protein," or a "fat" is. What is "overweight" or "underweight"? What does a healthy, moderate digital life look like?

Nietzsche offers us some answers to these questions. We should consume much of our information with deliberation, rather than as a morsel meant to be eaten as quickly as possible. We should bias ourselves toward the kinds of information worthy of this treatment—sustaining meals, not potato chips. We should digest this information well, metaphorically "chewing the cud" through multiple readings or through engaged thought. We should evacuate what does not serve us, forgetting trivial or useless information. And we should fast regularly from information altogether so that we can discover our own thoughts and better appreciate information when we return from solitude.

Nietzsche, like Fadell, has doubts about simple prescriptions that apply to all. What matters is making information serve life—and if your information use actually empowers your creative goals, more power to you. Regimens such as "put your screens away one hour before bedtime" are fine as far as they go, but these are blunt instruments.

Nietzsche would rather we become artists of our own lives. True artists, he says, don't simply invent but are also masters of "rejecting, sifting, transforming, ordering." In a world of infinite content, we too need sharpen our capacities for selection and rejection—and we should treat those tasks as seriously as real artists do.

The information diet in this chapter advises us to resist a gluttonous world. Our devices make information quick, easy, and available on demand. These are great qualities in a snack—but sometimes we need a meal. And though we may learn something here from ascetics such as the young John Chrysostom, we need not limit ourselves to a diet of bread and salt.

Four

WISDOM WON
BY WALKING

"Sit as Little as Possible"

"WHO WANTS TO LIVE FOREVER?" SANG FREDDIE MERCURY in the Queen song of the same name, but the answer is obvious: everyone. And when you're facing the prospect of death, even bad options start to look pretty good.

So when the doctor at the Singularity Clinic shows you the price list for off-loading your consciousness to a machine, and you realize that your life savings fall $150,000 short of the Cate Blanchett–inspired android of your dreams, and that the only receptacle you can afford is an immobile beige workstation with a single 80-watt power supply—well, you lower your standards.

"It won't be *that* bad," you tell yourself as you sign the papers. "I mean, I won't be attending a lot of cocktail parties once I'm trapped in a metal box that looks like a desktop computer circa 1998—but I can still think! And if I think . . . then I am. And that's a whole lot better than death."

Panic hits as you realize that the drive over to the clinic was the last time you will ever smell fresh air. This is unfortunate because, thanks to the canning factory by the river, the fresh air smelled strongly of pureed pumpkin.

"Relax," you tell yourself as they wheel you into the pre-op room and begin shaving your head. "Rational thought is the great achievement of the conscious mind, and I can enjoy it for centuries—or until my new hardware mines enough bitcoins to upgrade into that Cate Blanchett android."

Electrode gel appears in industrial quantities. Your head is lubricated. Wires are attached at so many points that you look like some high-tech Medusa. You realize, as you catch your reflection in a silver supply cabinet, that the last "book" you read was a *Peanuts* comic collection.

"People seem to *like* thinking," you observe. "It's very pleasant. Ask any philosopher! Wait—perhaps I'll become a philosopher. *Peanuts* need not define me! It's not like I won't have time for deep questions. Maybe I'll write a book. I'll write fifty books! I won't stop writing until I win the Nobel Prize. Do they give Nobel Prizes to philosophers?"

"No," says one of the interface techs who overhears your mumbling. "They don't."

He leans over you, the fluorescent light casting stark shadows around his face as he says, in a classic bit of understatement, "Now this is going to feel a bit weird . . ."

And he flips a switch.

THIS IS NOT, it should be said, how Silicon Valley proponents of "the Singularity" think it's going to happen. That's fine.

They're probably right, too—because the Singularity is *never* going to happen.*

But the thought experiment of off-loading our consciousness into a computer lets us ask a fascinating question that has preoccupied many philosophers, including Nietzsche: Would we think the same way if we were just brains in a vat—or machines in a data center?

Nietzsche was absolutely convinced that the body matters—and not solely as a transport vehicle for the reasoning mind. Recall these lines from *Zarathustra*:

> Behind your thoughts and feelings . . . stands a powerful commander, an unknown wise man—he is called self. He lives in your body, he is your body. There is more reason in your body than in your best wisdom.

The rational mind, though clearly important to a scholar such as Nietzsche, is ultimately not the essence of "who we are." It is a faculty, arriving rather late in the evolutionary process, that sits atop the body and the senses and believes itself to be in charge—though in reality, it is baffled and buffeted by desires that are based in a biology it does not fully control.

Nietzsche complains about Socrates, described as the archrationalist. In Plato's *Phaedrus*, Socrates uses the metaphor of a chariot to describe his view of the human person. Reason drives the chariot; passions are the unruly horses that threaten to wreck

---

* If I am wrong about this, I ask any of my descendants reading this passage to devote their own Singularity-enhanced lives to the study of time travel so that they can come back and rescue me.

the ride unless controlled by the driver and his whip. Reason here is—or should be—firmly in control.

Nietzsche doubts this whole way of thinking. What matters more to his project is understanding human passions and drives, which he calls "instinct." Socrates's problem was that he posed "'rationality' *against* instinct," says Nietzsche. "'Rationality' at any price is a dangerous force that undermines life."

In Nietzsche's view, rationality is not "ruling" the passions, nor should it be at war with them. Such an opposition is a kind of illness. Nietzsche sought harmony between reason and passion—an arrangement that would keep Enlightenment rationality within its proper bounds. Instinct emerged from evolutionary cognition, and it shows us how to live. We must not simply bypass or quash it. As he says in *Twilight of the Idols*:

> Socrates was a misunderstanding. . . . The most blinding daylight; rationality at any price; life, bright, cold, cautious, conscious, without instinct, in opposition to the instincts—all this too was a mere disease, another disease, and by no means a return to "virtue," to "health," to happiness. To *have* to fight the instincts—that is the formula of decadence: as long as life is *ascending*, happiness equals instinct.

Here Nietzsche echoes older thinkers such as the Scottish writer David Hume. In his 1740 work, *A Treatise of Human Nature*, Hume famously attacks the old Socratic idea that reason controls the passions. Indeed, for him it is the other way round.

"We speak not strictly and philosophically when we talk of the combat of passion and of reason," Hume writes. "Reason is, and ought only to be, the slave of the passions, and can never pretend to any other office than to serve and obey them."

Reason, for Hume, is a schemer; its job is to get (and to justify) what the passions want. That is why he says, "It is not contrary to reason to prefer the destruction of the whole world to the scratching of my finger. It is not contrary to reason for me to chuse my total ruin, to prevent the least uneasiness of an Indian or person wholly unknown to me." In other words, reason will try to take you anywhere your passions want to go—even if that involves a trip to crazy destinations.

Nietzsche and Hume represent a tradition that restores instinct, passion, and emotion to a central role in human thought and life. Emotions are not mere "feelings" tacked on to thoughts; we experience the world with and through them. We even *think* with them.

This idea has been validated by modern psychological research. In his 2012 bestseller, *The Righteous Mind*, social psychologist Jonathan Haidt collects decades of studies to argue that "emotions occur in steps, the first of which is to appraise something that just happened based on whether it advanced or hindered your goals. These appraisals are a kind of information processing; they are cognitions." That is why "contrasting emotion with cognition is therefore as pointless as contrasting rain with weather, or cars with vehicles."

Haidt sides with Hume over Socrates and Plato. But not completely. "I have argued that the Humean model (reason is a servant) fits the fact better than the Platonic model (reason could and should rule)," Haidt writes. "But when Hume said that reason is the 'slave' of the passions, I think he went too far."

Even if nonrational drives power most of our actions, reason can, over time, feed back into and even alter our emotions and instincts. But those instincts are powerful. Changes in their direction only happen as part of a long-term process, which explains why out-arguing someone rarely convinces them on the spot. Reason may be a self-justifying faculty, but it is not *only* that. (Haidt compares reason to a rider steering an elephant; the elephant is too powerful to be jerked this way and that by the rider, but through continual pressure on the reins, the rider can gradually change the elephant's direction.)

Nietzsche seems most sympathetic to a Haidt-like view. He clearly disagrees that reason rules the roost, but neither is reason a total slave to instinct. The two work in harmony—but the body and its instincts are the stronger faculty. They are the "great reason," while the mind and its rationality are only the "little reason." ("Thoughts are the shadows of our feelings," Nietzsche says, "always darker, emptier, and simpler than these.")

This view of what it means to be human helps explain Nietzsche's emphasis on physical engagement with the world. To sit in a chair, thinking "rational" thoughts as Descartes did, misses so much of what it is to be human—but it *also misses so much of what it means to think.* The idea that fully orbed human rationality might easily run on computing hardware would be anathema to Nietzsche.

Matthew Crawford touches on these ideas in *The World Beyond Your Head.* "We think through the body," he writes after recapping recent work on embodied cognition, a discipline that

> puts the mind back in the world, where it belongs, after several centuries of being locked within our heads. The boundary of our cognitive processes cannot be cleanly

drawn at the outer surface of our skulls. . . . They are, in
a sense, distributed in the world that we act in.

Our biology matters. We are not just Cartesian thinkers,
blocking out the winter wind as we scrape our mind back to a
tabula rasa. We are not brains in vats. We are not software running in a data center. The real world cannot—and should not—
be evaded, minimized, or ignored. Our very thoughts depend
on our bodies and the world those bodies encounter.

Nietzsche makes this realization a key part of his philosophy.
He could hardly put the point more strongly than he does in this
statement, which we have already glanced at, from *Ecce Homo*:

> *Sit* as little as possible; give no credence to any thought
> that was not born outdoors while one moved about
> freely—in which the muscles are not celebrating a feast,
> too: all prejudices come from the intestines. The sed-
> entary life—as I have said once before—is the real *sin*
> against the holy spirit.

Or, as Nietzsche puts it more pithily: "Only ideas *won by
walking* have any value." The body matters too much to spend
our lives staring at screens, which may be why *joy* is not an emotion usually associated with digital technology. But again and
again, the language of *joy* permeates descriptions of movement,
even the basic act of walking.

From Nietzsche to Charles Dickens to C.S. Lewis, thinkers and writers have exulted in their strolls around Sils Maria,
their rambles along the lamplit streets of nighttime London, or
their tramps through the Oxfordshire countryside. But it was
Thoreau who best summed up the essential need to move. "I

think that I cannot preserve my health and spirits," he wrote, "unless I spend four hours a day at least—and it is commonly more than that—sauntering through the woods and over the hills and fields, absolutely free from all worldly engagements."

Digital technologies, whether by design or by accident, now take so much of our time yet require so little of our bodies. Technologies have their uses, but the dangers too are clear, and Nietzsche raises questions about how long we should spend away from the "real" world.

Real Love

Of course, to put it this way is provocative. It assumes that our devices and the information they provide are somehow less real than books, grapevines, and smelting plants. It assumes that using a smartphone abandons the world. It assumes that digital constructs are ones and zeros, that they exist in a separate realm called "cyberspace," that they constitute an "information super-highway"—but fundamentally they are not the "real world."

This assumption underpins much of the talk about bodies and technology; the body and the world are real, while the smart-phone and the Internet are unreal. (Or, perhaps, less real.) What we need is more reality in our lives. As Sherry Turkle puts it on the opening page of *Alone Together*, "Technology proposes itself as the architect of our intimacies. These days, it suggests substi-tutions that put the real on the run." Here digital technology functions as a replacement for the real, not as something real in its own right; it is simulation and simulacra.

In this view, you have a "real" connection with the person sitting across the dinner table from you but a less-than-real connection with the person typing words to you in a chat window. It is the attitude behind the online acronym "IRL"—In Real Life—which refers to things done away from the screen and keyboard. One is real, the other is a poorer substitute.

Not everyone agrees with this assessment, and we should think a little about what the actual harms of digital technology might be. Not to get too *Matrix*-y about it, but what is real, exactly?

Are the computer and the smartphone real? They are made of quarks and atoms like anything else. Do Internet communications live in some separate "cyber" world? They are simply electrical impulses and magnetic fields. Is someone who taps away at a texting app all evening disconnected from real people? After all, they are connected to flesh-and-blood humans in other locations.

The argument is easy to grasp: Everything is part of our one world, so it's no help to speak about the physical world and the online world as though the two are separate. On a planet where online activities, from dating to terrorist plotting, have "real-world" consequences, the argument is also hard to dispute.

For instance, though a writer such as Andrew Sullivan can describe his "distraction sickness" by saying, "Every hour I spent online was not spent in the physical world," this is clearly not true. Every hour that Sullivan has spent anywhere was spent in the physical world. Where else might it have *been* spent?

Once you start looking, it becomes hard to pinpoint where the "unrealness" comes in. This has led to pushback among those who dislike talk about the supposed virtues of the "real" world and the terrifying danger of the "unreal" Internet.

Nathan Jurgenson, a sociologist who went on to work at Snapchat, sees all this worry about "the real" as a pointless moral panic. People who talk about putting down their smartphones and going out to split logs instead are, he thinks, just virtue signaling. In his 2012 essay "The IRL Fetish," Jurgenson powders his musket and lets fly at people like Turkle and Sullivan:

> What a ridiculous state of affairs this is. To obsess over the offline and deny all the ways we routinely remain disconnected is to fetishize this disconnection. Author after author pretends to be a lone voice, taking a courageous stand in support of the offline in precisely the moment it has proliferated and become over-valorized. For many, maintaining the action of the collective loss of the offline for everyone else is merely an attempt to construct their own personal time-outs as more special, as allowing them to rise above those social forces of distraction that have ensnared the masses. "I am real. I am the thoughtful human. You are the automaton."

In his view, the online and the offline are both real. We should see them as "enmeshed" instead of as wholly separate spheres. Consider: Though we put our device in a pocket, we might still be pondering our most recent text and crafting a reply. Though hanging from a rope halfway up an indoor climbing wall, we might be focused less on our feasting muscles than on how pictures from the climb will look on Facebook. Life moves fluidly between online and offline. "The logic of social media follows us long after we log out," Jurgenson writes. "There was and is no offline; it is a lusted-after fetish object that some claim special ability to attain, and it has always been a phantom."

Well, sure. But this seems more like an indictment of a performative culture preoccupied with recording and broadcasting life. Jurgenson's essay doesn't consider that people might not *like* the constant feeling of performing their own lives for the benefit of social media viewers. It certainly is useless to fault the "online" world if you spend all your "offline" time thinking about it—but that might argue instead for cultivating a more Dionysian embrace of the present moment.

Jurgenson's argument goes off the rails, though, when he claims that people who want to embrace the "real" physical world beyond their screens have actually never had it so good.

> We have never appreciated a solitary stroll, a camping trip, a face-to-face chat with friends, or even our boredom better than we do now. Nothing has contributed more to our collective appreciation for being logged off and technologically disconnected than the very technologies of connection. The ease of digital distraction has made us appreciate solitude with a new intensity. We savor being face-to-face with a small group of friends or family in one place and one time far more thanks to the digital sociality that so fluidly rearranges the rules of time and space. . . . Never has being disconnected— even if for just a moment—felt so profound.

As humans, we are terrifyingly good at tuning out repeated stimuli, so contrasting feelings do heighten sensation. But this does not seem like an argument for embracing every contrast in order to feel something more powerfully. We feel our surging good health with profound gratitude after recovering from strep throat—but who would then invite illness?

Those who argue against "digital dualism" are clearly correct in one sense; there is no ontologically separate "cyberspace." Everything is real. What happens "there" affects us "here," and vice versa. But this argument misses the point. It doesn't address the sense so many of us have that online interactions feel *different*; if you were one of those who spent the recent pandemic fighting off "Zoom brain" after one too many videoconferences, you might know what I mean.

Over hundreds of thousands of years, humans have developed a delicate social sensitivity to everything from body position to scent to flared nostrils to physical proximity. Stand 6 inches closer to someone and you send a suggestion—perhaps of aggression or romantic interest. Perhaps you are a "close talker" in the *Seinfeld* sense. Perhaps the other person likes this; perhaps the other person does not. This is all much harder to judge—and some of these signals disappear entirely—when talking to someone with their webcam angled up at the inside of their nose.

Digital tools do not operate in a fully fitted way with our evolved instincts and social behaviors. Just as the telephone stripped away everything but the voice, online interactions have truncated other aspects of human connection. Our machine-mediated connections are powerful tools, and well worth keeping, but they also lack the full expressiveness of interpersonal interaction. This has its benefits, as everyone can attest who has taken their cell phone into the bathroom during a conference call, but it won't satisfy the *fullness* of our need for connection.

That connection takes place in a world that has evolved under many pressures and thus to serve many purposes, but digital tools are tailored to appeal only to *us*. This is true of human tools in general, of course, but most of those tools require us to use them in (and against) the physical world. We shovel out a post hole or drive cars down country lanes, but digital technology reduces this "in-the-worldness" to the bare minimum: me, alone, and largely immobile.

Removing all that external friction means that digital tools can be precisely designed to stimulate our brains' pleasure centers. The "real world" offers no resistance here, as it does to the shovel or the car tire, until perhaps we start craving a quesadilla. As Cal Newport, the computer scientist, puts it, "Computer interfaces, and the increasingly intelligent software running behind the scenes, are designed to eliminate both the rough edges and the possibilities inherent in directly confronting your physical surroundings."

But the friction of the world, its independence from and resistance to our human plans, is not solely a source of frustration. It is also a challenge and a teacher. We test ourselves against the world beyond us, finding out through the snapping of a maple branch and the sharp sensation of being winded exactly how gravity works, how much load a tree can bear, the way certain objects flex before breaking, and the height of drops we can survive. Fixing a tire swing to that same tree calls forth that knowledge and presents it to our creative mind as a problem worth solving. Solving it correctly brings the unique satisfaction of a job done right, a pride in craft, and the scent of rubber in the summer sun. The knowledge we gain here is quite different from the same knowledge expressed in physics formulas, but it does bring with it the danger of standing atop a ladder, the possibility of bees, and a second aggravating trip to the hardware store because the carriage bolt you bought the first time was the wrong size.

Highly engineered digital spaces, though they may offer education and encourage creativity, don't do so in the same *physical* way. What we get is constant mental stimulation—from texting, from following one more link, from playing one more round of *Candy Crush*—that is so much more immediate in its gratifications than sunshine and an old tire. Marry this engineering to social media, with its metrics about likes and shares, and our identity can seem at stake online in a way it may not in the backyard.

In such crafted spaces, "the natural world begins to seem bland and tasteless, like broccoli compared with Cheetos," writes Matthew Crawford. "Stimulation begets a need for more stimulation; without it one feels antsy, unsettled. Hungry, almost."

Today this engineered activity comes to many of us through the single screen of the smartphone. Although the hardware, the cell towers, the backhaul fiber optics, and the people using the system are all part of the one "real world," I don't think it's so difficult to see how a screen-mediated approach to contemporary life might feel somewhat . . . different.

Different here is not code for "worse"; looking at the amounts of time people spend with their devices, it's clear that digital diversions are perceived as *better* than the analog, offline world. They offer a concentrated experience where we can reach anyone and learn anything and feel endlessly entertained without any of the downtime we encounter IRL.

In this sense, our engineered digital reality feels like utopia—the ideal of stimulation and novelty. Such utopias have always been a part of human dreams, whether we're talking about our longing for heaven or Plato's longing for the Forms. Those dreams all construct "other worlds" different from the actual one we inhabit. If used in the wrong way, these other worlds may entice us away from full participation in this one.

Nietzsche abhorred this common feature of our human predilections. Other worlds can serve many purposes, such as encouraging selfless behavior here and now, but Nietzsche distrusted them all as a dangerous form of escapism. He talks about this repeatedly across many books, but a short passage from *Twilight of the Idols* sums up the thought:

To invent fables about a world "other" than this one has no meaning at all, unless an instinct of slander, detraction, and suspicion against life has gained the upper hand in us: in that case we avenge ourselves against life with a phantasmagoria of "another," a "better" life.

This may sound extreme (surprise!), but I'm not sure Nietzsche is wrong. Perhaps, like me, you find yourself picking up your phone or cracking open your laptop as a sort of restless instinct. It's not from boredom—many of us have too many things going on, too many options, to actually be *bored*—and it may not happen for any particular reason. The most minute of hassles, the most microscopic of delays, even a pause in conversation and our attention shifts to the device.

In these moments are we not, in some sense, *slandering life*? We crave a level of novelty and stimulation that the world rarely offers, and we show through our actions that we don't really think that much of life's pace. We are ungrateful for what has been given. In small doses, this may not cause problems. But if we mainline digital stimulation, it's not hard to see how this attitude becomes a subtle—but pathological—rebuke to the world. *We know better.*

In opposition to this attitude, Nietzsche conducted his great experiment in *amor fati*, the "love of fate." He wanted to become a Yes-sayer who stopped worrying about life's unfairness, who did not brood over past slights, who accepted what the world doled out. One does not get to pick and choose; everything, in some mysterious sense, is ultimately all right. Even suffering and death are part of the pattern.

Nietzsche did not completely succeed in this. In *Ecce Homo*, after a lengthy passage berating his friends who didn't bother to study his writings, Nietzsche complains that "ten years have elapsed, and no one has yet felt it a duty to his conscience to defend my name against the absurd silence beneath which it has been entombed."

This does not sound like a man at peace with whatever happens to him, but Nietzsche suddenly seems to remember that petty personal slights are not *supposed* to bother him. He adds, unconvincingly, "For my part, these things have never caused me any pain; that which is necessary does not offend me. *Amor fati* is the core of my nature."

Amor fati sits uneasily beside Nietzsche's call to creatively transcend oneself. Accepting every horror that life can dole out might sound like a recipe for quietude rather than self-overcoming—the poor and the colonized putting up with the depredations of the rich and the strong. It's fate!

But Nietzsche is not commending "resignation" even to evil. He encourages us to change our lives and the world, while at the same time accepting our creature-ness and our limits without resentment. This can be a tricky tightrope to walk, but Nietzsche is saying something much like comedian Stephen Colbert, who has reflected on the plane crash that killed his father and two brothers back in 1974. "It's a gift to exist, and with existence comes suffering. There's no escape from that," Colbert said in a 2019 interview. To be grateful for one's life means "you have to be grateful for all of it. You can't pick and choose what you're grateful for."

This is the attitude Nietzsche tried to adopt. If he sometimes sounds like a man trying to convince himself of something, we shouldn't hold that against him. Nietzsche's suffering and personal failures humanize this man who liked to present himself as a solitary sage hiding behind a mustache, drinking his weak tea, and plotting the self-overcoming of the species from affordable rented rooms.

Have we wandered beyond the borders of a book concerned with technology? If so, the diversion may be a useful one. We need not accept *amor fati* as Nietzsche tried to live it out, but we might absorb something of his attitude—a sense that, though we strive creatively against life's limits, we are *not running away*.

We can say Yes to this life, to remaining in the moment with people, to letting our thoughts trail off into boredom, and we can find a certain sturdy joy in experiencing the world as it offers itself to us. We may find at the end of it all that subtler pleasures, often ones beyond our screens, are the ones that endure.

This is not a commandment but perhaps a useful principle by which we judge for ourselves whether our technology use has become . . . unreal.

The ~~Triumph~~ Weakness of the Will

Let's grant that we want to engage our fully evolved human-ness in and against the given world. We want more than keyboards and glass. But arriving at this conclusion does not necessarily translate into less screen time—in part because "willing" ourselves to do something is hard. Tired, bored, hungry, sad, or just yearning to "swipe right" on Tinder? If you have trained yourself to find novelty, entertainment, or dating partners through your phone, you will have to resist the urge to start tapping away at it—regardless of any mental resolutions to the contrary.

If reason sits atop our passions, habits, and instincts like a rider atop an elephant, it cannot succeed by simply asserting dominance; the elephant is far too powerful. Perhaps the rider can jerk the reins hard enough to compel a slight change of direction, but the effort fatigues us.

But cheer up: Reason is a crafty rider, and what it can't quickly get through sheer force of will, it might attain through guile. When it comes to altering behavior, reason works better when it can structure reality in advance instead of relying on constant "in the moment" decision-making.

When you go to Gran-gran's on Sunday afternoons to play Scrabble and eat shortbread cookies, you *could* consciously decide not to check your phone every time it blorks and beeps. You might just, you know, *tune it out*. But, if you are anything like me, your mind can't stop wondering about which fascinating people might be texting you. What life-changing communications lie behind that lock screen? You may think Gran-gran doesn't notice your distraction, but she does—and she is silently judging you from behind her Scrabble tray.

You are more likely to keep your attention where you want it if you silence your phone's notifications, turn it off during your shortbread-munching visit, or even leave it at home for a few hours. You have shaped the environment for a shot at success. Is this a simple, fleeting trick played on our habits? Not necessarily. We may find over time that such external tweaks to our situation actually change our internal desires.

Nietzsche believed strongly that change works on us from outside in, actions influencing our feelings. Many of our "chronic illnesses of the soul . . . are very rarely due to one gross offence against physical and mental reason," he writes, "but as a general rule they arise from innumerable and petty negligences of a minor order." Therefore, fixing these interior illnesses may be accomplished by making practical changes "even in his least important habits." Matthew Crawford, who has written much about skilled practices and craft, notes a similar discovery: "Habit seems to work from the outside in; from behavior to personality."

Lofty ideals about *taking action in the world* are fine, but the energy to take that action may be missing if we sit for 12 hours a day, don't exercise, and skip breakfast. Can something as trivial as a bagel with a side of scrambled eggs cure our souls?

The point of a book like this one is not only to encourage certain mental conclusions about the role of technology in our lives; it is to shape our practices so that they embody these conclusions. Here are a few approaches for shaping yourself and your environment in ways that help you venture out into the world.

STRETCH YOUR ATTENTION SPAN.

Paying attention is a skill. Given the ways gadgets can hobble our ability to focus, it's useful to build consciously "attentional" time into the weekly schedule. This might involve anything from board games to books, bird-watching to worship.

Reading is perhaps an obvious place to start, because so many people complain today about the loss of the pleasure they once took in books. Additionally, it is inexpensive, often enlightening, and it requires nothing more exotic than a chair, a cozy lamp, and a cup of tea. (You can read on a tablet or smartphone, but given the ease of distractions, it's less recommended for trying to improve one's capacity for attention.)

Keep doing what you're doing until you feel that tug of distraction—then push beyond it for 5 or 10 minutes more. Start small and fail often. It took me a year of sustained reading to recover my ability to read deeply.

NOTE DIFFERENCES BETWEEN DIGITAL
AND ANALOG WORK.

Perhaps you, like me, are occasionally *particular* about small things. These preferences may drive your parents, spouse, or friends batty, but you aren't trying to be difficult; you just know that little things matter. You also know that your preference is objectively correct. If others can't see that, it's their loss.

If I'm brainstorming crazy ideas for a book on Nietzsche and technology, I can't use ruled paper. It's not possible. All those horizontal lines lock me into complete sentences, when I still need wild and fragmentary freedom. Blank paper works in a pinch, but my loudest mental thunderclaps form on a specific brand of colored graph paper, crisply printed in Spain, with 5-millimeter grid spacing and microperforations down the side for clean removal. It offers structure without constraint. Writing on it—using a Pilot G-2 fine-point pen, naturally—is a tactile and aesthetic pleasure.

I am aware of how precious this sounds.

But the paper matters. Brainstorming on a computer has a completely different feel, and I don't get the same results. I need the freedom to make lists here and there, to draw wild lines between them, to circle and to highlight, to doodle in the corners as I think. I need to run my hand over the page, to feel ideas flowing out through ink. I need that most sublime of sensations—the pleasure of blotting out a terrible idea with vicious pen strokes of disdain.

The digital and the analog worlds are not isometric with one another, even when it appears that the same activity is being performed. In something as simple as a word processor, which appears to mimic the blank page, we can quickly sense a difference.

Scholar and critic Alan Jacobs gets at this difference in several of his theses regarding technology. He illustrates his point by discussing handwriting. He argues that:

- Everyone should sometimes write by hand, to recall what it's like to have second thoughts before the first ones are completely recorded.
- Everyone should sometimes write by hand, to revisit and refresh certain synaptic connections between mind and body.
- To shift from typing to (hand)writing to speaking is to be instructed in the relations among minds, bodies, and technologies.

Pay attention to these sorts of differences. Write a card by hand and take it to a co-worker's office rather than sending an email. Do your next PowerPoint presentation with a large paper flipboard instead—and draw all the art in black Sharpie. Call the library for directions rather than using the GPS.

The point is not to see how the analog way is "superior"—it may not be—but to understand the qualities of each approach. How does each way of doing things affect you? Other people? The world around you?

ENGAGE IN SKILLED ACTIVITY.
Take your expanded attention span and apply it to skilled practices where you must develop both creativity and technical acumen. Find something that you can do outside of work that is refreshing. Take watercolor lessons, learn to brine a ham, pick up the flute, practice dovetail joinery, bake your own sourdough bread, go ballroom dancing, strap on some ice skates.

In the past few years, for instance, I have taught myself to play bass guitar, to install new Shimano click shifters on my daughter's bike, to paint on 140-pound cold-pressed paper, to compose guitar instrumentals, to skim coat a wall, to dance with my wife. Each activity required more than mere attention; it required certain tools or certain skills, and each had its frustrations, but I have never regretted a moment of this time. In the end, I exerted effort against the world to create sound or watercolor paintings or gorgeously smooth drywall, and this felt productive in a way that consuming, watching, and purchasing rarely does.

Technology can be an amazing partner here; it is often terrific for learning skilled practices. The return of "artisanal" everything may have emerged out of a sense that industrialization has destroyed the unique—Nietzsche complains about this at some length—but sites such as YouTube now offer on-demand expertise in everything from drawing a laughing avocado to fixing the sink drain that *someone* installed incorrectly. With the skills listed above, technology played an important role in each, whether that involved how-to videos, composition software, online courses, or the music lessons I took via videoconference during the pandemic.

One caveat: If you are a knowledge worker and spend your day staring at a screen, perhaps don't start with a sedentary, screen-based project such as writing the first great novel about Michigan's Upper Peninsula. Yes, it's skilled and creative work, but it also feeds into the same postures and habits of the workday. The goal here is to test yourself in new ways against the world, to use the body differently, and to improve the world or your own life through creation or maintenance. Whatever you do, you'll make Nietzsche proud.

CULTIVATE COMMUNAL FOCAL PRACTICES.

Albert Borgmann, the Montana professor and philosopher of technology, has written for decades about the "device paradigm" under which we live. His most famous example involves the hearth, which for many centuries created the main focal point of a house. The hearth provided heat, which in colder climates naturally gathered the family. It also provided space and energy for cooking. In doing so, it dictated family roles across a day: Father might chop wood in the morning, while mother did the cooking in the evening, and children might be called upon to keep the indoor woodpile stocked. The family gathered around the hearth for meals and an evening's relaxation. Domestic bliss?

But hearths require hard work. Someone has to rise in the chill of the morning to start the fire. Splitting logs by hand, which I once attempted at a "living history" farm, is more difficult than it looks—and much more likely to injure you. Ash has to be constantly removed from the fireplace; sparks have to be watched. Bats and birds might fly down the chimney even as creosote builds up inside it.

Long ago we replaced the hearth with central heating. The furnace does not sit at the center of the home; instead, you must descend rough stairs to the back of the basement, where the heating apparatus lies entombed in its windowless room. The "device paradigm" values ends more than means, so all the "means" are hidden in the walls. We hear only whispers of air blowing through vents; we see only a thermostat mounted on the wall.

With this change, the "focal" property of the hearth was broken. Furnaces do not require family jobs, daily routines, and physical exertion. They do not require the same skill to use. And they do not bring people together. In fact, by efficiently heating all parts of all rooms, they make it much easier for family members to disappear into separate spaces.

Borgmann worries that our embrace of the device paradigm has removed the need for skill and craft from too many parts of our lives. In doing so, the device paradigm has leached meaning from life; we feel somewhat deadened. Borgmann advocates a recovery of "focal practices" that we value for their own sake, things such as gardening, reciting poetry, making and sharing meals, fishing, writing letters. These overlap with the skilled activity discussed earlier, but the key here is that they demand our concentrated attention. So far, so Nietzschean.

But Nietzsche, the lonely individualist, dances on the heights as he looks down at the "herd" in the valley. We have seen how this perspective can be used to call people to excellence, though it may be a lonely or elite achievement. Borgmann, however, worries about too much individualism. He is especially concerned about the ways in which technology isolates us in our cars, our cubicles, our homes, our bedrooms—perhaps even on our respective sides of the bed, where two people tap away on their iPhones in the late evening.

So Borgmann places great stress on *communal* focal practices such as the evening meal, the sharing of stories in a pub, musical performances. Such practices do more than put people into proximity with one another; they knit together the attention offered by each participant to create something meaningful for the group. These practices benefit from the same kind of scaffolding and structure we have been discussing; willpower "in the moment" cannot by itself pull a collection of people into a shared activity.

Consider the dinner table. Even after the physical hearth faded in focal importance—though note how many living rooms remain oriented around a rarely used fireplace—the "evening meal" tradition gathered families daily. This meal is common enough that we may not even think of it as a tradition. It sounds simple. Do we not just sit down and eat? But dining together has its share of rules and rituals: particular times; the use of certain vessels, plates, and utensils; the call to be seated; the washing of hands; perhaps a prayer or a thanksgiving; a procession of courses; the washing up.

For this communal focal event to take place, customized spaces and objects are required. A kitchen collects counter and cooking space, ingredients, and knowledge (recipes and cook-books). Cupboards keep our plates and pots near at hand; the silverware is in the drawer; the table and chairs stand ever ready. But even with these specialized arrangements, the focal event does not take place without daily *practice*. We take action, and we take it repeatedly, to turn this collection of spaces and objects into a profound focal activity.

It might be simpler in every way to microwave frozen meals and eat them in front of the TV; it might be easier; it might even be more *fun*. But it might not be as rewarding.

What can we do to create spaces in our lives that bring people out of their comfortable, technology-created cocoons and help them focus their attention in shared experiences that create and sustain communities? The answers will vary wildly by location and life situation, but structure matters here. One-off attempts to bring people together are terrific, but they also take a terrific toll in terms of energy and effort.

If you want to bring family members together around musi-cal creation, create a space that makes it likely. You don't need a wood-paneled music studio, just a corner of the living room with a digital keyboard, a djembe, maybe a guitar. Throw in a music stand and store chord charts or songbooks on the bookshelf. You've just lowered the barrier to entry—in under a minute, people can start playing.

As with the evening meal, however, the best preparations may lead to haphazard results without regular practice. Planning ahead is not always popular, but "text me when you want to play, and I'll see if I'm free" is less likely to produce good results.

SEEK LESS CONTROLLED SETTINGS.

Did I get annoyed when attending a Josh Ritter concert where I had to sit through a 1-hour opening act I could have done without? Absolutely. Were expletives silently directed at the person in front of me who simply could not stop talking between songs? Possibly. Did I pound my hand on the steering wheel when an overturned truck shut down the exit ramp I needed to get home? No comment. But what I gained was an experience not reproducible on my far more convenient couch at home.

Nietzsche tells us to look skeptically at the easy, controlled life, while our devices beckon with their total control over what we see, what we hear, and how we communicate. If we have become control freaks, we should seek situations that we cannot fully manage. This does not need to involve ecstasy, dance music, and an abandoned warehouse. Start small—even a face-to-face conversation can be difficult for those with social anxiety who might prefer the time for thought offered by texting and email.

Why attempt to make our peace with a world we cannot control? Because this is the fundamental reality, one merely masked by our devices. The control that they offer us feels significant but is of such a limited kind. In life's less predictable moments we can encounter the sorts of surprising experiences—both good and bad—that are less likely to occur in the world that we have ordered.

TAKE CHARGE OF YOUR DEVICE EXPERIENCE.

The big tech companies now recognize the lifestyle problems that accompany their best-selling devices, and all of them offer tools to help. Take advantage of notification and "do not disturb" settings on your phone. Consider "full screen mode" on your laptop to avoid distractions or switch off the WiFi for an hour while you complete a project. Close email when you're doing something else. Pick up an app that blocks time-wasting websites during certain hours—and let a friend set the password. Remove apps that soak up your time. Use the tools provided by companies such as Google and Android to manage your digital well-being and to track your screen time.

The goal is reducing the workload on your willpower. Set up the scaffolding around your digital life so that it directs you by default in the directions you want to go and blocks off paths you know aren't good for you to follow. In this way, you can up the odds that your use of digital devices will be intentional rather than haphazard and distracting.

SET DEVICES ASIDE.

Finally, if you want to encourage more interaction with the world, find times to set your devices aside. Just as we discussed fasting from information, consider fasting from the devices through which we access and process that information.

I survived an entire childhood of rides in a Chevy station wagon with a rear-facing "third seat," which we generally used without seatbelts. The car had a cassette player but no air conditioning, so it was difficult to *hear* any music over the sound of wind whooshing through the open windows at highway speeds. Our GPS was a decade-old road atlas.

I made it through two decades of this savagery—so I can probably make it 4 hours without carrying an electronic tether around. You can too.

Our devices as not as essential as they want us to think, and the world is not always as dangerous as we fear.

The Body Is Not a Battery

Imagine a software engineer, just out of college, who is bent on retiring by age 35. In pursuit of this dream, she works hundred-hour weeks. She has slept at her desk three times this year, but she knows the importance of caring for her body. She starts each day with a nutritionally complete shake mixed with a raw egg—not because she *likes* the taste of artificial vanilla, but because it is an efficient way to down enough calories before her morning commute.

Stiff at the end of a long day spent in a chair, she has developed a pain in her "mousing" shoulder and recently began yoga at her company's gym. On non-yoga days, she swims. She would rather spend Sunday afternoon napping on the couch, but she dutifully gets up each week and jogs along the lakeshore to keep her heart in shape. "Gotta stay healthy," she tells you.

(Were you imagining California? *For shame.* She lives in Wisconsin. She's proud of Wisconsin! And she can't stand people who assume that everyone who knows how to program a computer has migrated to San Francisco. Wait until you hear her rant about how much further one's housing dollar goes in the Midwest.)

She ends each day with a cup of tea and a book; no screens, because she worries that the blue light keeps her awake.

Good for her! But also, in a way, maybe not so good for her? Alicia—yes, her name is Alicia—has embraced her embodied-ness—but only as a means to an end. Her body is a machine, and like all machines, it needs a certain amount of maintenance. But the goal of this maintenance is, like most maintenance, about keeping the machine *working*. How easily Alicia has become a creature of productivity, even as her ultimate goal is escaping the daily grind.

Nietzsche questions this orientation toward work. Where are the joys of the body *for their own sake*?

> Oh, this moderation in "joy" of our cultured and uncul-
> tured classes! Oh, this increasing suspiciousness of all
> enjoyment! *Work* is winning over more and more the
> good conscience to its side: the desire for enjoyment
> already calls itself "need of recreation," and even begins
> to be ashamed of itself. "One owes it to one's health,"
> people say, when they are caught at a picnic. Indeed,
> it might soon go so far that one could not yield to the
> desire for the *vita contemplativa* (that is to say, excursions
> with thoughts and friends), without self-contempt and a
> bad conscience.

What we want to avoid is seeing the body as a recharge-able battery that exists to keep the mind going. This would be to disregard the wisdom of the body and to treat it merely as a means to a more productive end. And there's little joy in such an approach.

The Return of Dionysus

You and I are not in the habit of having infants torn to pieces,
but this was the sort of jealous nonsense that the Greek gods
lived for. Dionysus was one of many children spawned by the
philandering Zeus, and Zeus's wife Hera was displeased. She
revenged herself on the child, who was dismembered and then
eaten. Grisly stuff! But Dionysus wasn't *quite* dead.

Here's how the staid *Encyclopedia Britannica* tells one version
of the tale:

> Dionysus—under the name Zagreus—was the son of Zeus
> by his daughter Persephone. At the direction of Hera,
> the infant Zagreus/Dionysus was torn to pieces, cooked,
> and eaten by the evil Titans. But his heart was saved by
> Athena, and he (now Dionysus) was resurrected by Zeus
> through Semele. Zeus struck the Titans with lightning,
> and they were consumed by fire. From their ashes came
> the first humans, who thus possessed both the evil nature
> of the Titans and the divine nature of the gods.

(Still exciting! There's no way to keep a good dismember-
ment story down.)

The rending and resurrection of Dionysus took on signifi-
cance among some Greek mystery religions. Dionysus became
a symbol of original unity being torn into individual pieces,
then re-created as a unity. This is what Nietzsche means when
he says, in *The Birth of Tragedy*, that the mystery religions taught
"the basic understanding of the unity of all things, individuation seen as the primal source of evil, art as the joyful hope that

the spell of individuation can be broken, as a presentiment of a restored oneness."

Over the course of his work, Nietzsche becomes an arch-individualist, but he never abandons the idea that we moderns too easily lose our connection to primal reality. Our temptation, colored by the lens of our technology, is to say that we are separate from the animal passions, from the cruelty of the killer whale playing with the baby seal before biting it in two. We convince ourselves that we are masters of our desires, but Nietzsche's genealogical investigations remind us how much a part of this evolving world we are.

Living among rational Apollonian types who could no longer escape their own heads, Nietzsche seeks a return to oneness with the world. "This hope alone casts a ray of joy across the face of the world, torn and fragmented into individuals," he says.

In a preface written years later, he scoffed at his own book. "Today I find it an impossible book," he says. "Badly written, clumsy and embarrassing, its images frenzied and confused, sentimental" and "lacking in any desire for logical purity."

But the fact that *The Birth of Tragedy* has endured for more than a century tells us how much the ideas have spoken to people. (Well, the ideas in the first half, anyway. The second half, with its praise of Wagner, is widely regarded as rubbish.)

Nietzsche is not against thought, reason, or Netflix. But he sees the way our post-Enlightenment age has made it easy to reason, to watch, and to worry our way through life. We operate at a remove from the world.

Our digital devices are part of this trajectory. They provide a constant stream of individualized interruptions and on-demand distractions that feed our minds, at the expense of our muscles. They isolate us heads-down from one another. They insist on the screen's priority to mediate reality. And in doing so, they often show elements of arrogance. "Today our whole attitude towards nature," Nietzsche complains, "is one of hubris, our violation of nature with the aid of machines and the thoughtless ingenuity of technicians and engineers."

Nietzsche, the former classics professor, challenges this info-heavy, arch-rationalist way of living. Head knowledge is not always the pathway to self-knowledge, and thought is not the only way we seek and find reality. In the preface to *On the Genealogy of Morals*, Nietzsche quotes Jesus's own words:

> We are unknown to ourselves, we men of knowledge—
> and with good reason. We have never sought ourselves—
> how could it happen that we should ever *find* ourselves? It
> has rightly been said: "Where your treasure is, there will
> your heart be also."

Nietzsche, Borgmann, Crawford, Jacobs—they all suggest, in different ways, that too much treasure has been gifted to our technology, which is not worthy of it. Our hearts can be found in our cars, our televisions, our smartphones, or scattered into bits across the Internet.

But we too easily forget what the body teaches us about the joy it takes in the world. We are not brains in vats; we are not made to live as androids. We are part of the world in all its pain, and we show our creativity and we test our strength against its resistance. In running, in eating, in making love, in mastering a craft, in maintaining a focal practice, in paying true attention to another, we lower the volume of the Apollonian voice inside us—and we turn up the Dionysian.

"I think, therefore I am"? Sure. But also: "I act, therefore I am."

Five

THE GAY SCIENCE?

The Greatest Weight

AS A DIGITAL SELF-HELP GURU, NIETZSCHE IS A BIT OF A bummer. He thunders against the safe and easy life. He advocates information restriction and the power of forgetting. He calls for the skillful exertion of our bodies against the world, even when we'd rather put our feet up on the coffee table and eat a pot of mac and cheese while watching cat videos on YouTube.

But just wait until you peer into the hellmouth of the "eternal return." It is one of Nietzsche's most famous and strangest and *heaviest* ideas. Which is saying something, coming from a guy who advocates suicide so that each of us can die on our own terms. The best-known version of eternal return appears in *The Gay Science*, book 4, section 341, as an aphoristic little story called—appropriately—"The greatest weight."

What if one day or night a demon came to you in your most solitary solitude and said to you: "This life, as you now live it and have lived it, you will have to live again, and innumerable times again, and there will be nothing new in it; but rather every pain and joy, every thought and sigh, and all the unutterably trivial or great things in your life will have to happen to you again, with everything in the same series and sequence. . . . The eternal hourglass of existence will be turned over again and again, and you with it, you speck of dust!"

Would you not throw yourself down and gnash your teeth and curse the demon who spoke to you thus? Or was there one time when you experienced a tremendous moment in which you would answer him: "You are a god, and I have never heard anything so divine!" If that thought took hold of you as you are, it would transform you and perhaps crush you; the question with regard to each and every thing, "Do you want this again, innumerable times again?" would weigh upon your actions with the greatest weight! Or how well disposed would you have to become to yourself and to life, that you might *long for nothing more* than this final eternal confirmation and seal?

The idea is based on the conjecture that there are a limited number of states in the Universe; the number may be incomprehensibly large, but it remains finite. If the Universe itself is of infinite duration, however—as Nietzsche seemed to think it might be—every arrangement of matter and energy could eventually occur again. And again.

In his notebooks, Nietzsche tried to work out scenarios in which science might support the "eternal return" of all things. Scholars today argue about whether he believed in eternal recurrence as a physical reality, but I don't find the question all that interesting. Whether he did or not, in his published works the idea operates as a thought experiment designed to make us look carefully at our own lives. In that sense it continues to have value today.

We often have fantasies of returning to some younger age. *If only I knew then what I know now!* The fantasies always imagine how much sharper our decisions, how much higher our self-confidence, how much better our hairstyles would be.

Nietzsche says "No!" to this habit of mind. We must accept and integrate the events of our lives even when they are not ideal; this is *Amor Fati 101*. This is difficult enough, but the idea of eternal return makes such acceptance so much harder. Not only do we have to accept our life, with all its imperfections and limits, once—we have to accept the same life an infinite number of times. Is the way I will spend my time today, this week, this year bearable were it to repeat forever? Can I truly say the ultimate Yes to *every single action I am about to take?*

If this sounds paralyzing, Nietzsche understands. What life could measure up? How could we make even the smallest of decisions with this as the standard? The eternal recurrence lies upon us like a tombstone slab. It is "the greatest weight." And it can crush us.

Yet it can only crush us *as we are*, and Nietzsche has little interest in what we are; he wants to see *what we can become*. As we've seen, the self-overcomer, the transformed human, the *übermensch* becomes "well disposed" toward existence—and thus can embrace even the eternal recurrence.

Most of the time, I'm in the "throw yourself down and gnash your teeth and curse the demon who spoke to you thus" camp when it comes to eternal return. The sheer cognitive load sounds exhausting. Trying to decide, each time I eat a bowl of chocolate ice cream, if this is an event I can accept an infinite number of times gives me a pain, which I alleviate by eating more chocolate ice cream.

But the "eternal return" remains a powerful—if occasional—positive stimulus. How easily we sink into the hot tubs of our lives and relax there for far longer than the posted 15-minute limit. Asking ourselves whether the lives we lead are lives we are proud of, whether they are lives in which we are growing into richer and deeper humanity, is a crucial question. It's the one Nietzsche poses to us here.

"Do you want this again and innumerable times again?" whispers the demon. Some of us, should we cultivate the mental space required to hear our most solitary solitude, might answer: "No." We have given too much power—too much *time*—to our screens, and it is hard to will the eternal return of the "last man."

This book describes a Nietzschean alternative. But here, as we near the end of our contemplation, one thing needs to be faced: Change is going to hurt.

The Cure and the Disease

"Where are the new physicians of the soul?" Nietzsche asks in aphorism 52 of *Daybreak*.

He is looking back over the history of human need: our need for meaning, for transcendental purpose, for an explanation of suffering. He sees these longings as a collective sickness that we have battled for millennia. Animals appear free from it, yet we suffer mightily. The medicine we have used against this sickness varied widely: religion, philosophy, even the modern distractions of industrial consumerism or overwork. But these medicines, in Nietzsche's view, too often encouraged us to seek

"another world" in heaven, in Platonic Forms, in Socratic reason, in hedonism, in distraction. In different ways, the cures
dealt with our hunger for meaning by pulling us away from
the full reality of our place in this world—a risky place that
we inhabit as embodied creatures with evolved emotions and
instincts, but one where we can still overcome ourselves and
advance the range of human possibilities. Such cures may actually make us more ill once their effectiveness wanes.

> The worst disease of mankind has arisen from the strug-
> gle against diseases, and apparent remedies have in the
> long run brought about worse conditions than those
> which it was intended to remove by their use.
>
> Men, in their ignorance, used to believe that the stu-
> pefying and intoxicating means, which appeared to act
> immediately, the so-called "consolations," were the true
> healing powers: they even failed to observe that they had
> often to pay for their immediate relief by a general and
> profound deterioration in health, that the sick ones had
> to suffer from the after-effects of the intoxication, then
> from the absence of the intoxication, and, later on, from
> a feeling of disquietude, depression, nervous starts, and
> ill-health.
>
> Again, men whose illness had advanced to a certain
> extent never recovered from it.

The obsession with which we use our digital devices—their
omnipresence in so many waking lives—suggests that they are
more than merely entertaining. Some deeply felt need is being
met or perhaps avoided. We clearly see our devices as a remedy—for something.

Yet our "cure" often looks like acute dependency. Intoxi-cated and then anesthetized by screens, we depend on them to provide everything from friendship to sex to entertainment. Still, large numbers of people express at least vague dissatisfac-tion with lives mediated so heavily by screens. In the quiet of our "loneliest loneliness," a life dependent on screens may feel too thin, like the ice on a frozen lake over which we have skated out quite a ways. Will it hold us? Then we look at all the other skaters on the ice, and we doubt our initial concern. Everyone seems to be having such a grand time. Perhaps if we just glide a little closer to shore, where the ice is thicker, we can keep skat-ing as before.

Maybe we can. But Nietzsche's final challenge to us asks whether a thorough re-fashioning of the self can be accom-plished with only gentle tweaking around the edges.

Nietzsche got irritated about many things, from having to buy silk underwear for Wagner (really) to the number of thun-derstorms that rumbled over Sils Maria in the summer. But his greatest source of agitation was the German culture he had left behind. In his view, Germany wanted to keep its traditional practices and habits of mind while abandoning the beliefs that had produced them in the first place. But this is no good. Old consolations and enjoyments must be surrendered; you can't simply smuggle them into a new paradigm.

The digital paradigm active in many wealthy societies today stresses:

- constant entertainment
- physical safety
- control
- continual and worldwide connection with others

- unlimited information
- "another world" rather than my local, physical world
- mental stimulation over physical activity

If we become skeptical of where this paradigm has taken us, then our actions should reflect our changed beliefs. In some facets of our digital lives, moderation and sensible limits may be enough; that is, dialing back our screen usage by 30 percent and picking up the guitar might offer enough change to satisfy. But there might be other areas in which even moderated behavior still feels unhelpful—social media has been an area of common complaint, as have streaming video services. Perhaps podcasts take too much of your time; perhaps you read far too much online news about events and ideas that don't really affect you. Some of these may demand renunciation.

Nietzsche recognized that such a life might not offer everything, but he thought it could offer enough. People too often let themselves be used by technology and by its creators: used not as human beings but "as the screws of a machine and the stopgaps, as it were, of the human spirit of invention." This happens in part because people feel that they always need more money—and they need more money because they have "accustomed themselves to many wants." But freedom can be found if we can "unlearn some of these wants!" To retain our independence from the world of the machine, we must rediscover "a philosophy in rags" and "the freedom of spirit of a man who has few needs."

Rags and relinquishment. Whatever criticisms we might make of Nietzsche, he lived what he wrote. He gave up the bourgeois trappings of success. He walked away from his university chair. He lived modestly on a small pension, he never owned a home, he had almost no property. His books were his only children—and no one read them while he was sane enough to care. But living as he did allowed him to exercise his deep convictions about a life oriented to creative thought rather than to financial "productivity."

I am not excited about the idea of wearing rags, even metaphorically, but Nietzsche is right not to let us off too easily with inspiring slogans and incremental tweaks. If we seek real treatment from new physicians of the soul, it can't all be painless.

The Lightest Feet

How crushing all this can sound— the eternal return, our "most solitary solitude," fasting, renunciation, the new physicians of the soul. To return for a moment to our metaphor of nutrition, is life itself nothing but kale and wheatgrass?

Nietzsche can be hyperbolic to make a point, and he is widely seen as a dour thinker whose painful life ended in madness. But Nietzsche was fundamentally convinced that joy was possible through a great Yes-saying to life. One cannot run away into other worlds, no matter how compelling such distractions may be, but to live in *this* world is not meant to be a burden. When he speaks of well-lived human lives, Nietzsche speaks often of dancing, laughter, and play.

"I know of no other way of dealing with great tasks than that of *play*," he writes in *Ecce Homo*. "This is, as a sign of greatness, an essential precondition. The slightest constraint, the gloomy mien, any kind of harsh note in the throat are all objections to a man, how much more to his work!"

This attitude was not a product of his incipient madness; one sees it everywhere in his mature work. In his *Zarathustra* days, Nietzsche says he can "only believe in a God that would know how to dance. And when I saw my devil, I found him serious, thorough, profound, solemn: he was the spirit of gravity—through him all things fall." What is true of gods goes also for men. "All good things laugh," Nietzsche says. "The gait betrays whether one is truly striding along one's *own* path: so watch me walking! But whoever is approaching his goal—dances."

This is why Nietzsche named one of his books *The Gay Science* (sometimes translated as *The Joyful Wisdom* or *The Joyous Science*). He found a way out of his personal crisis after leaving his Basel professorship, and it was, despite all his sufferings, a way of joy—a way of Yes.

We can look to his personal life, however, to see that the real Nietzsche was much less rigid than the authorial voice of his books.

Take information overload. Nietzsche clearly delights in tweaking his former university colleagues with comments on how he avoids books, how he only rereads eight authors, and how reading prevents him from hearing his own voice. He certainly believed these things as general principles, yet he in fact read widely—and he did not limit himself to his small personal canon. This was how he discovered one of his favorite authors, the French writer Stendhal, who was discovered through sheer serendipity. "Stendhal is one of the happiest accidents of my life," Nietzsche says, "for everything that marks an epoch in it has been brought to me by accident and never by means of a recommendation." Nietzsche was not just about restriction and rereading; he had an openness to happenstance and luck.

Or consider his diatribes against sitting still. In reality, Nietzsche spent much of his time in a chair or on a bed, whether due to illness or simply to his love of conversation—when he could get it. On a visit to one of his few good friends, the church history professor Franz Overbeck in Basel, Overbeck's wife says that Nietzsche would often drop by for "hours" at a time. He would eat nothing but "lightly brewed tea and a few English cakes," and he would sit "on the sofa in my husband's study or on a certain armchair in the living room, with his back to the white stove, looking at my husband, who sat opposite him, or at the dark curtain."

Like Jesus, who told his followers to pluck out their eyes if those eyes led them astray, Nietzsche was a hyperbolist. His parables and aphorisms demand a response from readers, stir them up, provoke—but his attacks on old orthodoxies should not be read as new rigidities.

As we try new things, Nietzsche says, "we are always finally recompensed for our good-will, our patience, reasonableness and gentleness towards what is unfamiliar, by the unfamiliar slowly throwing off its veil and presenting itself to us as a new, ineffable beauty. That is its thanks for our hospitality. He also who loves himself must have learned it in this way; there is no other way. Love also has to be learned."

Joy, dancing, laughter, goodwill, patience, play, and beauty. Nietzsche is not, in the end, a downer, and the things he wants from life are surprisingly upbeat. But before we close, there is one serious limit to his thought: Nietzsche was dancing and laughing and playing *alone*.

Forever Alone

Nietzsche's father, Pastor Carl Ludwig Nietzsche, died in 1849. Friedrich was only 5 at the time, and his life became a cloistered one among a mother, a sister, and several live-in aunts. Later in life, he would write blistering letters to his mother and sister, at one point cutting off contact with them completely. He felt sick whenever they nagged at him or asked too many questions; he tried hard to shake free of their influence.

This need to pull away from others marks his whole life. In *Ecce Homo,* Nietzsche notes how far back in his biography it goes. "At an absurdly tender age," he writes, "in fact when I was seven years old, I already knew that no human speech would ever reach me: did any one ever see me sad on that account?"

As with many statements that Nietzsche makes about his own feelings, this last one is impossible to take at face value. In his private letters, Nietzsche refers to himself as "the hermit of Sils-Maria" and complains repeatedly about the pain of isolation.

In 1876, when his friend Erwin Rohde got engaged, Nietzsche wrote about marriage. "Things are different with me, heaven knows, or, perhaps, does not know," he says. "To me all this does not seem so necessary,—except on rare days."

Those "rare days" were not all that rare; Nietzsche talks several times about suicidal feelings, including after his estrangement from the woman he loved most passionately, Lou Salomé. In 1882, after she ran off with one of Nietzsche's friends, Nietzsche wrote the pair of them an extremely pathetic letter.

"Even if I should, by chance, yielding to some impulse or other, take my life, there would not be too much to be sad over," he says. "Ponder on this very carefully that, in the last analysis, I am touched in the head, half ready to be confined to the lunatic asylum, totally confused by my long loneliness." He took a tremendous dose of opium "out of despair."

Ida Overbeck, the wife of Nietzsche's friend Franz, saw Nietzsche shortly after the breakup, when he returned to Basel to lick his wounds. "So then I really am going into complete solitude," Nietzsche told her when he left. He did not say it with relish.

And in 1884, when Rohde sent him a picture of his young daughter, Nietzsche replied with a note about his own lack of connections. "Oh, my friend," he said, "what a frantic reticent life I am living! So alone, so very much alone! So without 'children!'"

This isolation illuminates a key feature of his philosophy: an anger against others that leads to a disdain for society, for place, for rootedness. His philosophy of restless adventure comes, in part, from a place of pain. In 1885, Nietzsche told his mother and sister that he might visit them—but only if the meeting was *not* in his childhood home of Naumburg. The place "does not agree with me and has not a thing that finds response in my heart," he wrote. "I was not 'born' there and never felt as if I were at 'home' there."

In *Human, All Too Human*, Nietzsche erupts at the powerful internal awakening that comes when one turns one's back on "home."

> "Better to die than live *here*," so sounds the imperious and seductive voice. And this "here," this "at home" is everything which it had loved until then! A sudden horror and suspicion of that which it loved; a lightning flash of contempt toward that which was its "obligation"; a rebellious, despotic, volcanically jolting desire to roam abroad, to become alienated, cool, sober, icy: a hatred of love, perhaps a desecratory reaching and glancing *backward*, to where it had until then worshiped and loved; perhaps a blush of shame at its most recent act, and at the same time, jubilation *that* it was done . . .

Nietzsche could not feel himself part of a community. All he could see was how such things hold us back. "Who today still feels a serious obligation to bind himself and his descendants to one place?" he asks, foreshadowing his own restless wandering about Europe. But Ida Overbeck saw the pain behind this imagery of strength with her insightful comment: "Nietzsche hated the normal person because he could not be one."

Nietzsche writes like a man running away from something. As much as he wanted to say Yes to the world, he never found a people among whom he could be fully comfortable. In the end, he retreated into solitude—alone with his writing, where he could conjure up the world he wanted in place of the world as it was.

In the opening passages of *Human, All Too Human*, Nietzsche admits this; the "free spirits" of which he writes do not in fact exist, he says; he has been forced to invent them because of the friends he lacks.

Nietzsche's visions are profound, but they skew individualistic and libertarian. They skew toward solitude. They skew, in an odd way, toward control. To follow wholly in Nietzsche's footsteps would re-create some of the problems we see in our current technological moment: the danger of solipsism, alone with the tools we control, connecting to people more through words than through personal presence.

"Technology is seductive when what it offers meets our human vulnerabilities," writes Sherry Turkle in *Alone Together*. "And as it turns out, we are very vulnerable indeed. We're lonely but fearful of intimacy. Digital connections and the sociable robot may offer the illusion of companionship without the demands of friendship. Our networked life allows us to hide from each other, even as we are tethered to each other."

Life online can take us anywhere. We can meet anyone; we can *become* anyone. This ability to remake ourselves can be especially valuable to marginalized or isolated people, but only if we find new communities with which to engage. We don't always do this, though. Confronted with the uncomfortable, we can "ghost" friends and lovers, we can delete emails, we can click away to the next forum, the next chat room, the next Tinder match. Like Nietzsche, we may even celebrate our "freedom." But "when people talk about the pleasures of these weak-tie relationships as 'friction free,'" Turkle writes, "they are usually referring to the kind of relationship you can have without leaving your desk."

The "herd" of humanity can cause us great suffering, as it did in the "chain sickness" Nietzsche felt when bound to his mother and sister. But creative risk-taking means continuing the search for a community of wholeness and health. Nietzsche couldn't find it, and he seems to have given up on the idea. In a world driven mad by loneliness and isolation, we must not.

We noted in the first chapter that Nietzsche is worth thinking with—but not always worth rigid devotion. Seeing him alone up there on the "heights," gazing down with contempt on the herd in the valley, we might feel a touch of compassion for the lonely dancer of the snows.

Nietzsche would have hated this—but he would have supported our right to critique him. As Nietzsche scholar Richard Schact notes in his introduction to *Human, All Too Human*, "Distinguishing between genuine insights and personal preferences, prejudices, over-generalizations, irresistible puns and other such inspirations is not easy. . . . But by precept and example [Nietzsche] invites us to subject him to the same sort of scrutiny to which he subjects others; and that is something many will want to do."

Nietzsche himself said something similar in an 1878 letter: "Followers I do not want. May each man, or woman, be only *his,* or *her,* true disciple!"

In my view, the most productive way to read Nietzsche is Nietzschean. That is, we can accept many of his goals, such as creative self-overcoming, the restriction of other voices, and the need to engage the physical world with the body. I find Nietzsche both provocative and persuasive on these matters.

But if Nietzsche could see what many of us can't, perhaps we can see something Nietzsche couldn't: These goals are often accomplished in community. I could not live a life of creative struggle if I was cut off from my family and my children, my friends and my church, my culture and my country. Who would I be struggling *for*? Myself alone? My fellow solitary genius *übermenschen*? What a depressing thought.

Nietzsche correctly diagnosed the need for joy in an industrializing world, where life and work felt commoditized and flattened. He demanded something more human. He called us to "become who we are" and to say Yes to life. But his will to power wasn't balanced by a will to love—which provides fuel for the healthiest kind of risk-taking.

Screens can too easily swallow our lives. They disrupt our local experiences tens or even hundreds of times per day. They pour information out in such quantities that we spend our working lives touching and tapping—and our resting evenings sitting and staring.

We will never extricate ourselves by simply saying No. Our screens are too useful for that. What we need to tame their overreach is a better Yes, and that Yes will involve the joy and the love found in intimate connections. Sex and friendship, shared meals and sweaty softball leagues, board games and beers, fishing with

friends and family road trips—in remaking our lives, we would
do well to remember the *community* that Nietzsche forgot.

The Eye of the Tiger

One step at a time, I walked away from that life which had
become too small for me. I am still walking. Whether I will ever
"arrive" feels less important than embracing the becoming-ness.
It is a lesson that Nietzsche taught but which I have followed in
my own way. He would most certainly not approve of my path,
but he might appreciate the journey.

Nietzsche pushes us toward a goal-driven life of creative
excellence, the use of attention to foster deep wisdom rather
than superficial "knowledge," and embodied life at play in the
world. All this is to be done with the light touch of joy, not the
great weight of duty.

Nothing said in this book should be construed as "against
technology." We cannot go back to some mythically wonderful
pre-technological age, but we cannot go on as we have, either.
As Nietzsche put it in a quote we saw in the first chapter:

> We are faltering, but we must not let it make us afraid
> and perhaps surrender the new things we have gained.
> Moreover, we cannot return to the old, we have burned
> our boats; all that remains is for us to be brave, let hap-
> pen what may.—Let us only go forward, let us only
> make a move!

As we say our Yes to the world, we will gain clarity about
how our devices and services can be tamed for our health and

the health of those around us. We don't do this out of any hatred toward technology, but out of the sense that there are other goods in life being squeezed out by our inventions. As the philosopher Albert Borgmann writes in his 1984 classic, *Technology and the Character of Contemporary Life*, reforming the role that technology plays in modern life "does not stem from ill will toward technology but from the experience that there are forces that rightfully claim our engagement and truly grace our lives." We cannot always access these forces through technology; indeed, to do so is often "to eviscerate them."

Sometimes this reformation takes modest forms. But at other times, we must take more dramatic action. In the midst of true emergencies, we may find ourselves, like Nietzsche, philosophizing with a hammer. As we tap with increased force and urgency, sounding out the false idols in our lives and cultures, we should not be surprised to find ourselves, at least occasionally, breaking some glass.

As for me, it took time to read well once more—full-length books, on paper, with a pen in hand. Then I learned to reread. I gave away much of what I had previously gathered when I realized I had no *need* to go through it a second time.

I joined a group of friends who were deep into modern board-gaming, which was about as far from the *Monopoly* and *Life* of my childhood as it was possible to get. We gathered over kitchen tables for years, transmuting cards and cardboard into relationships. We took weekend retreats together. We shared new game discoveries like explorers back from strange lands.

I kept paper to-do lists. I bought a weather station. I muted my phone. I deleted most of my past email and half of my photos. I bought a used bass and a new acoustic guitar. I began composing music. I played flute and guitar duets with my daughter.

I took up painting. I began to move: yoga classes, bodyweight training, long bike rides through sweaty summer nights. And I wrote this book.

But what I really learned from Nietzsche was the need for a *well-risked life*. Safety, in the end, won't save you; to live your life well, you must be prepared to lose it. So my family and I risked that ease and comfort by selling our home and moving across the country to pursue new dreams and new communities. Were these the right decisions? Are there such things as "right decisions"? I have no idea. Yet they were risks taken with enough care that I can embrace them as Nietzsche embraced his own *amor fati*. The boats have been burned, and we can only fare forward.

I owe Nietzsche a debt of thanks, 125 years on from his own suffering, because I am no longer—well, not always—the "second-to-last-man." On my best days, screens now take on a servant's role; on my worst, they still command my gaze like an idol. But I find it slightly easier now to look at the world and not away from it. In small but important ways, I am rising from the couch and stepping back into a creative life—sporting the Eye of the Tiger.

Reader, will you join me?

A NIETZSCHE READING LIST

Nietzsche's own output was massive, and the secondary literature can be overwhelming. In this brief guide, I offer some suggestions for Nietzsche newcomers interested in learning more.
Works by and then about Nietzsche are arranged in a suggested
reading order. (If you already have a background in Nietzsche's
work, anything on these lists should be intelligible.)

Twilight of the Idols

Written near the end of Nietzsche's sane life, this short volume
distills his key themes into something likely both to provoke
and baffle many first-time readers of Nietzsche. My advice: Start
here but pass over anything that is initially unclear; if you return
to *Twilight* after reading several other Nietzsche works, it will all
(well, mostly) make sense.

Thus Spoke Zarathustra

Yes, its pastiche of the Bible and self-help exhortations can
produce some truly over-ripe prose at times, but there's a reason this is so popular. *Zarathustra* remains the closest thing to a
novel that Nietzsche ever wrote, and the language throughout

is invigorating. I guarantee this is like no philosophy book you have ever read. It contains extended discussions of the *übermensch* and the "last man," along with plenty of parables that will be hard to interpret without some kind of annotation or explanation.

On the Genealogy of Morals

Three more traditional essays that show Nietzsche's "genealogical" method at work. He traces several hallowed concepts—such as pity and asceticism—back to their (imaginatively reconstructed) roots to show that the ground they emerged from was "human, all too human." It is a provocative read that talks at length about "master" and "slave" morality.

Daybreak. The Gay Science. Human, All Too Human.
Beyond Good and Evil

All four of these are "aphoristic" works that cover a wide range of topics. The first three are sometimes known as the "free-spirit" trilogy of Nietzsche's alleged "middle period," while *Beyond Good and Evil* has more links to later works such as *On the Genealogy of Morals*. Still, any one of these is a fine introduction to Nietzsche's aphoristic style, though I personally gravitate toward *Daybreak* and *The Gay Science* (perhaps the most personal of the four). Because they cover some of the same thematic and stylistic ground, I would pick one of them and move on, returning to the others later if interest remains.

Ecce Homo

A highly idiosyncratic "autobiography" that Nietzsche wrote weeks before his insanity. Though traces of megalomania do appear in the book, it remains a beautifully written testament to what Nietzsche was trying to do with his life and writings.

The Birth of Tragedy. The Anti-Christ. The Will to Power. Untimely Meditations

Best suited for true Nietzsche devotees. .

The Birth of Tragedy's first half is fascinating, though you need to have a taste for arguments about Greek dramatists to get through it.

The Anti-Christ is a nearly hysterical polemic against Christianity—read the last few pages if you doubt this—and represents Nietzsche at his No-saying worst. Provocative, but *Beyond Good and Evil* and *On the Genealogy of Morals* make many similar points under far greater control.

The Will to Power comes from Nietzsche's notebooks and contains material explored but never published by him. For that reason, it remains tricky to use as a guide to Nietzsche's thought.

The *Untimely Meditations* are four long essays written when Nietzsche was a young professor. All are well crafted, though only the essay on history contains much of interest to nonspecialists today. Unless, that is, you like reading takedowns of David Strauss or puffery about Richard Wagner.

I Am Dynamite! A Life of Nietzsche. Sue Prideaux.

The newest of the Nietzsche biographies, this 2018 entry is also one of the best. It focuses more on Nietzsche's life than on his ideas, but it brings that life powerfully to life. It is especially good at using a carefully chosen selection of quotes from Nietzsche's books and letters. For instance, here's Nietzsche complaining about his illness: "This neuralgia goes to work so thoroughly, so scientifically, that it literally probes me to find how much pain I can endure, and each of its investigations lasts for thirty hours." Prideaux is a fine writer, and her book is certainly the most compulsively readable of the books on Nietzsche. It is perhaps the best place for Nietzsche newcomers to start.

Nietzsche: Unpublished Letters. Kurt Leidecker, translator and editor.

This 1959 book is well worth picking up at a library or used bookstore. It simply collects 75 letters that span Nietzsche's life. The first is from the schoolboy Nietzsche to his sister, Elisabeth, recommending to her specific books and some musical pieces by Schumann; the last is from the days after Nietzsche's insanity, when he wrote, "I had Caiaphas put in chains." Between those poles you can watch Nietzsche grow to maturity, struggle with his career, express his suffering and loneliness, show a touch of megalomania, and get into fights with this mother and sister. It is an intimate self-portrait of a complex man.

Conversations with Nietzsche: A Life in the Words of His Contemporaries. Sander Gilman, editor; David Parent, translator.

What did the young Professor Nietzsche wear around Basel? ("Light-colored pants, a short jacket, and around his collar fluttered a delicately knotted necktie, also of a lighter color.")

What was it like to hike with Nietzsche up Mount Boron in 1884? ("There I tasted for the first time the 'vermouth de Torino,' poured by Nietzsche, whom the mistral had stirred up into a most excited mood, full of humorous ideas," remembered one companion.)

What was Nietzsche like 8 years into his insanity? ("When

he was told music would be played, he immediately was ecstatic and emitted ugly, unarticulated sounds, a dull, horrible groaning. After the music began his whole face was transfigured and beamed indescribably.")

This book collects accounts of Nietzsche from those who knew him. It draws from essays and newspaper pieces published largely in German as Nietzsche grew famous during his insanity and then after his death. Endlessly illuminating, this is worth reading if you want to feel Nietzsche as a human being and not just as a "prophet." Highly recommended.

Nietzsche: The Man and His Philosophy.
R.J. Hollingdale.

This is a classic biography by one of Nietzsche's best translators. As the subtitle indicates, the book balances Nietzsche's story with his unfolding philosophical views. If it does not reveal the character and humanity of Nietzsche as well as Prideaux's book does, it remains a good one-volume overview of Nietzsche's life and thought—and well worth a read as a second Nietzsche biography.

The Philosophy of Friedrich Nietzsche.
Robert Solomon and Kathleen Higgins.

Not a book, this series of 24 half-hour lectures on Nietzsche comes from The Teaching Company and offers a terrific audio overview of Nietzsche's work. Solomon and Higgins are a pair of married professors at the University of Texas, and they team teach this college-level course. It largely ignores Nietzsche's biography to concentrate on the ideas, including the *übermensch*, asceticism, the Greeks, nihilism, *amor fati*, "immoralism," and rationality. Perfect for commuters or for gym use, this is a solid introduction to Nietzsche's thought in audio form.

Hiking with Nietzsche. John Kaag.

An American philosophy professor describes two of his own journeys to Sils Maria, in Switzerland, where he hikes the same walkways and mountain paths that Nietzsche hiked during his most fruitful period. Kaag's two trips, coming 18 years apart, aim to find out more about Nietzsche—but they end up revealing quite a bit about Kaag. Easy to read, with a nice sense of place, it illuminates both Nietzsche and the physical places he inhabited.

Nietzsche: Philosopher, Psychologist, Antichrist. Walter Kaufmann.

Kaufmann was a longtime philosophy professor at Princeton who had himself left Nazi Germany in 1939. He took great pains to show that Nietzsche was not a proto-Nazi, and with this book Kaufmann played a key role in rehabilitating Nietzsche in the English-speaking world after World War II. It leans perhaps too heavily on the idea of the "gentle" Nietzsche, and it's much harder going for casual readers than the Hollingdale or Prideaux biographies. But Kaufmann was an incisive thinker, and his long discussions of Nietzsche's key themes remain worth reading.

NOTES

A note on sources.

Titles. Nietzsche's books have been translated under different titles over the years. Some of these changes are minor, such as *Thus Spake Zarathustra* in old versions and *Thus Spoke Zarathustra* in modern translations. *Zur Genealogie der Moral* has been translated, with frustratingly minute differences, as *The Genealogy of Morals*, *On the Genealogy of Morality*, and *On the Genealogy of Morals*.

But some variations are more significant. One of Nietzsche's aphoristic works is called *Morgenröte* and has been published in English as *Dawn*, as *Daybreak*, and as *The Dawn of Day*. Another book, *Die fröhliche Wissenschaft,* is often translated as *The Gay Science*—in part due to Nietzsche's subtitle "la gaya scienza"—but it is also translated as *The Joyful Wisdom* and *The Joyous Science*.

I have drawn from many different translations of Nietzsche's works, but to keep things clear for readers, I will use only one title for each work in the main text: *Daybreak, Thus Spoke Zarathustra, On the Genealogy of Morals,* and *The Gay Science* are the main beneficiaries of this policy. The notes will indicate which specific translation was used for each quotation, however.

Masculine language. Nietzsche's language is often explicitly masculine. Altering it comprehensively would have meant reworking many passages and would probably distort the feeling—both good and ill—one gets from reading Nietzsche. I have elected to leave the language in place when it appears in quotes. In my own words, I have attempted to be gender neutral.

One: Burn the Boats

3   *"Americans consumed information"*: See the UCSD press release announcing details of the study athttps://ucsdnews.ucsd.edu/archive/newsrel/general/12-09Information.asp.

7   *"that famous hollow sound"*: Friedrich Nietzsche, *Twilight of the Idols and The Anti-Christ*, trans. R.J. Hollingdale (London: Penguin Books, 1968), 31.

7   *"If we possess our why of life"*: Nietzsche, *Twilight of the Idols and The Anti-Christ* (Hollingdale trans.), 33.

9   *As a 14-year-old*: Sue Prideaux, *I Am Dynamite: A Life of Nietzsche* (New York: Tim Duggan Books, 2018), 27–29.

9   *"At Pforta they were treating Nietzsche's ghastly episodes"*: Prideaux, *I Am Dynamite*, 36.

11   *"If the enduring homeland of this good life"*: Friedrich Nietzsche, *Human, All Too Human*, trans. Marion Faber and Stephen Lehmann (London: Penguin Books, 1994), 170.

12   *"Small, soft, round, unending sand"*: Friedrich Nietzsche, *Daybreak*, trans. R.J. Hollingdale (Cambridge: Cambridge University Press, 1982), 106.

13   *"If you experience suffering and displeasure as evil"*: Friedrich Nietzsche, *The Gay Science*, trans. Walter Kaufmann (New York: Vintage Books, 1974), 270.

16   *"The time has come for man to plant the seed"*: Friedrich Nietzsche, *Thus Spoke Zarathustra*, trans. Walter Kaufmann (New York: Modern Library, 1995), 17.

17 *Nietzsche thinks it equally likely*: Nietzsche, *Thus Spoke Zarathustra* (Kaufmann trans.), 17.

17 *"Nietzsche regards the failure to draw a distinction"*: From Michael Tanner's introduction to *Twilight of the Idols and The Anti-Christ* (Hollingdale trans.), 11.

17 *"The earth has become small"*: *Thus Spoke Zarathustra* (Kaufmann trans.), 17–18.

18 *"Give us this last man, O Zarathustra"*: *Thus Spoke Zarathustra* (Kaufmann trans.), 18.

19 *"Information has become a form of garbage"*: Neil Postman, *Technopoly* (New York: Alfred A. Knopf, 1992), 69–70.

20 *"The discovery of new worlds"*: Ann Blair, *Too Much to Know* (New Haven, CT: Yale University Press, 2011), 11.

21 *"Even if all knowledge could be found in books"*: Quoted in Blair, *Too Much to Know*, 5.

21 *"A diminution of that tension of feeling"*: Friedrich Nietzsche, *Human, All Too Human*, trans. Helen Zimmern, vol. 1 (London: George Allen and Unwin, 1909), 227.

22 *"Ten years behind me"*: Friedrich Nietzsche, *Ecce Homo*, trans. R.J. Hollingdale (London: Penguin Books, 1991), 61.

22 Yet he cannot shake his *"tormenting feelings"*: Friedrich Nietzsche, *Untimely Meditations*, trans. R.J. Hollingdale (Cambridge: Cambridge University Press, 1983), 60.

23 *"We need history, certainly"*: Nietzsche, *Untimely Meditations* (Hollingdale trans.), 59.

24 *"Perhaps we philosophers, all of us"*: Friedrich Nietzsche, *The Joyful Wisdom*, trans. Thomas Common (Edinburgh: T.N. Foulis, 1910), 350.

25 *"put an end to all book-wormishness"*: Friedrich Nietzsche, *Ecce Homo*, trans. Anthony Ludovici (New York: Macmillan, 1911), 88.

25 *"That nethermost self"*: Nietzsche, *Ecce Homo* (Ludovici trans.), 88.

25 *"I moved out of the house of the scholars"*: Friedrich Nietzsche, *Thus Spoke Zarathustra*, trans. Graham Parkes (Oxford: Oxford University Press, 2005), 108.

28 *"huge and mighty forms that do not live"*: William Wordsworth, *The Pre-*

lude: Or, Growth of a Poet's Mind (Oxford: Oxford University Press, 1970), 12.

29   *"We do not belong to those who have ideas only among books"*: Nietzsche, *Gay Science* (Kaufmann trans.), 322.

30   *"Sit as little as possible"*: Friedrich Nietzsche, *Basic Writings of Nietzsche*, trans. Walter Kaufmann (New York: Modern Library, 1992), 695–96.

31   *"that restraining boundary"*: Friedrich Nietzsche, *The Birth of Tragedy*, trans. Shaun Whiteside (London: Penguin Books, 1993), 16.

31   *"Not only is the bond between man and man"*: Nietzsche, *Birth of Tragedy* (Whiteside trans.), 17.

31   *"These poor creatures have no idea how blighted"*: Nietzsche, *Birth of Tragedy* (Whiteside trans.), 17.

32   *Socrates was a "typical decadent"*: *Basic Writings of Nietzsche* (Kaufmann trans.), 727.

32   *Nielsen data from 2019*: Shown in the 2019 edition of Mary Meeker's well-known "Internet Trends" report. Mary Meeker, *Internet Trends 2019*, https://www.bondcap.com/report/itr19/#view/38, slide 38.

33   *"The ties we form through the Internet"*: Sherry Turkle, *Alone Together* (New York: Basic Books, 2011), 280.

35   *"By an excess of effort"*: Friedrich Nietzsche, *Human, All Too Human*, trans. Paul Cohn, vol. 2 (New York: Macmillan, 1911), 34.

35   *"the cultivation of a mental stance without objects"*: Alan Jacobs, "Attending to Technology: Theses for Disputation," *New Atlantis* 48 (Winter 2016): 23. Also available online (no page numbers) at https://www.thenewatlantis.com/publications/attending-to-technology-theses-for-disputation.

36   *"I knew noble people who lost their highest hope"*: Friedrich Nietzsche, *Thus Spoke Zarathustra*, trans. Adrian Del Caro (Cambridge: Cambridge University Press, 2006), 31.

38   *"The weak and ill-constituted shall perish"*: Nietzsche, *Twilight of the Idols and The Anti-Christ* (Hollingdale trans.), 128.

38   *"The sick man is a parasite of society"*: Friedrich Nietzsche, *The Portable Nietzsche*, trans. Walter Kaufmann (New York: Penguin Books, 1982), 536.

39   *"We can assent to no state of affairs"*: Nietzsche, *Ecce Homo* (Ludovici trans.), 42.

39   *"I have just had all anti-Semites shot!"*: Quoted in R.J. Hollingdale, *Nietzsche: The Man and His Philosophy* (Cambridge: Cambridge University Press, 1999), 238.

41   *"There is plenty in each of these books"*: From Richard Schact's introduction to Friedrich Nietzsche, *Human, All Too Human*, trans. R.J. Hollingdale (Cambridge: Cambridge University Press, 1986), xxii.

41   *"As always in reading Nietzsche"*: From Michael Tanner's introduction to Nietzsche, *Daybreak* (Hollingdale trans.), xiii.

41   *"There are cranky reflections on diet and climate"*: From Bernard Williams's introduction to Friedrich Nietzsche, *The Gay Science*, trans. Josephine Nauckhoff (Cambridge: Cambridge University Press, 2001), xi–xii.

42   *"bathos, sentences that invite quotation out of context"*: Nietzsche, *Portable Nietzsche* (Kaufmann trans.), 2.

42   *"I mistrust all systematizers"*: Nietzsche, *Twilight of the Idols and The Anti-Christ* (Hollingdale trans.), 35.

42   *"We are faltering, but we must not let it make us afraid"*: *Human, All Too Human* (Hollingdale trans.), 118.

43   *"There is no work of Nietzsche's"*: Nietzsche, *Basic Writings of Nietzsche* (Kaufmann trans.), xiv.

Two: The Secret of My Happiness

45   *"Human nature has on the whole been changed"*: Friedrich Nietzsche, *The Joyful Wisdom*, trans. Thomas Common (Edinburgh: T.N. Foulis, 1910), 35.

46   *"We thirsted for lightning and action"*: Friedrich Nietzsche, *Twilight of the Idols and The Anti-Christ*, trans. R.J. Hollingdale (London: Penguin Books, 1968), 127.

46   *"In a journey, we commonly forget its goal"*: Friedrich Nietzsche, *Human, All Too Human*, trans. Paul Cohn, vol. 2 (New York: Macmillan, 1911), 297.

48 *"For at the sight of work"*: Friedrich Nietzsche, *The Dawn of Day*, trans. J.M. Kennedy (New York: Macmillan, 1911), 176–77.

48 *"Leisure in the age of work"*: Robert McGinn, "Nietzsche on Technology," *Journal of the History of Ideas* 41, no. 4 (1980): 688.

49 *"distracted from distraction by distraction"*: T.S. Eliot, *Four Quartets* (New York: Harcourt, Brace & World, 1943), 17.

49 *They were told to "entertain themselves with their thoughts"*: Timothy D. Wilson, David A. Reinhard, Erin C. Westgate, et al., "Just Think: The Challenges of the Disengaged Mind," *Science* 345, no. 6192 (2014): 76, https://wjh-www.harvard.edu/~dtg/WILSON%20ET%20AL%20 2014.pdf

50 *"If the 'why' of one's life is clear"*: Friedrich Nietzsche, *The Will to Power*, trans. R. Kevin Hill and Michael Scarpitti (London: Penguin Books, 2017), 444.

51 *"At bottom, I find those moral codes distasteful"*: Friedrich Nietzsche, *The Gay Science*, trans. Walter Kaufmann (New York: Vintage Books, 1974), 196.

51 *"Ever since there have been human beings"*: Friedrich Nietzsche, *Thus Spoke Zarathustra*, trans. Graham Parkes (Oxford: Oxford University Press, 2005), 76.

52 *Every creature, Nietzsche argues, "instinctively strives"*: Friedrich Nietzsche, *On the Genealogy of Morals and Ecce Homo*, trans. Walter Kaufmann and R.J. Hollingdale (New York: Vintage Books, 1967), 107.

52 *"at the extension of power"*: *Joyful Wisdom* (Common trans.), 289–90.

53 *"Friedrich Nietzsche said that joy is the feeling"*: Matthew Crawford, *The World Beyond Your Head* (New York: Farrar, Straus and Giroux, 2015), 52.

54 *technology is "a product of the highest intellectual energies"*: Friedrich Nietzsche, *Human, All Too Human*, trans. R.J. Hollingdale (Cambridge: Cambridge University Press, 1986), 366–67.

54 *Too many of the "energies" unleashed*: Nietzsche, *Human, All Too Human*, vol. 2 (Cohn trans.), 210.

55 *"the proliferation of intriguing technological innovations"*: McGinn, "Nietzsche on Technology," 689.

56 *"The development and use of certain technologies"*: McGinn, "Nietzsche on Technology," 690.

57 *"We all live, comparatively speaking, in far too great security"*: Friedrich
Nietzsche, *Daybreak*, trans. R.J. Hollingdale (Cambridge: Cambridge
University Press, 1982), 192.

58 *"It is the misfortune of active men"*: Friedrich Nietzsche, *Human, All Too
Human*, trans. Marion Faber and Stephen Lehmann (London: Penguin
Books, 1994), 170.

58 *"For lack of rest, our civilization"*: Friedrich Nietzsche, *Human, All Too
Human*, trans. Helen Zimmern, vol. 1 (London: George Allen and
Unwin, 1909), 260.

59 *"The man who has become free"*: Nietzsche, *Twilight of the Idols and The
Anti-Christ* (Hollingdale trans.), 104.

60 *"Nietzsche did not intend to prescribe warfare"*: Paul Zweig, *The Adventurer:
The Fate of Adventure in the Western World* (Princeton, NJ: Princeton
University Press, 1974), 219.

60 *"To modestly embrace a small happiness"*: Friedrich Nietzsche, *Thus Spoke
Zarathustra*, trans. Adrian Del Caro (Cambridge: Cambridge University Press, 2006), 135–36.

61 *"And this secret life itself spoke to me"*: Nietzsche, *Thus Spoke Zarathustra*
(Del Caro trans.), 89–90.

62 *"The strongest legacy of iGen'ers' involvement"*: Jean Twenge, *iGen* (New
York: Atria Books, 2017), 177.

63 *"Our networked life allows us to hide"*: Sherry Turkle, *Alone Together* (New
York: Basic Books, 2011), 1, 157.

64 *"For—believe me—the secret for harvesting"*: Friedrich Nietzsche, *The
Gay Science*, trans. Josephine Nauckhoff (Cambridge: Cambridge University Press, 2001), 161.

64 *"And if you must perish"*: Nietzsche, *Dawn of Day* (Kennedy trans.), 316.

65 *"Shy, ashamed, awkward, like the tiger"*: Friedrich Nietzsche, *Thus Spake
Zarathustra*, trans. Thomas Common (Mineola, NY: Dover Publications, 1999), 209.

65 *"He who has always much indulged himself"*: Nietzsche, *Thus Spake Zarathustra* (Common trans.), 104.

66 *"Repeatedly [Nietzsche] insists that 'knowledge'"*: Zweig, *The Adventurer*,
205.

66 *"In order to make this point"*: Zweig, *The Adventurer*, 205–6.

68 *"Their song of 'equal rights' "*: Nietzsche, *Joyful Wisdom* (Common trans.), 343.

68 *"may in a certain rough sense become good manners"*: Friedrich Nietzsche, *Beyond Good and Evil*, trans. R.J. Hollingdale (London: Penguin Books, 1990), 193–94.

71 *"The windmill gives you society"*: Karl Marx, *The Poverty of Philosophy* (Chicago: Charles H. Kerr, 1913), 119.

71 *"Embedded in every tool"*: Neil Postman, *Technopoly* (New York: Alfred A. Knopf, 1992), 13.

71 *"The press, the machine, the railway"*: Nietzsche, *Human, All Too Human* (Hollingdale trans.), 378.

73 *"People don't succumb to screens"*: Cal Newport, *Digital Minimalism: Choosing a Focused Life in a Noisy World* (New York: Portfolio/Penguin, 2019), 9.

74 *"The world might conceivably avoid destruction"*: From Bernard Williams's introduction to Nietzsche, *Gay Science* (Nauckhoff trans.), xiii–xiv.

75 *Apollo is a god who "conceals nothing and says nothing"*: Friedrich Nietzsche, *Untimely Meditations*, trans. R.J. Hollingdale (Cambridge: Cambridge University Press, 1983), 122.

76 *"How can anyone become a thinker"*: Nietzsche, *Human, All Too Human* (Hollingdale trans.), 390.

76 *"the most general defect in our methods of education"*: Nietzsche, *Dawn of Day* (Kennedy trans.), 319.

77 *"Behind your thoughts and feelings"*: Nietzsche, *Thus Spoke Zarathustra* (Del Caro trans.), 23.

77 *"I say, let us first and foremost have works!"*: Nietzsche, *Dawn of Day* (Kennedy trans.), 29.

78 *"Inspired by the Nietzschean ideal of human excellence"*: McGinn, "Nietzsche on Technology," 691.

Three: The Information Diet

79 *Palladius says that his "gastric regions were deadened"*: Quoted in J.N.D. Kelly, *Golden Mouth* (London: Duckworth, 1995), 31–33.

80 *"The ascetic treats life as a wrong road"*: Friedrich Nietzsche, *On the Genealogy of Morals and Ecce Homo*, trans. Walter Kaufmann and R.J. Hollingdale (New York: Vintage Books, 1967), 117.

80 *"I do not want to accuse"*: Friedrich Nietzsche, *The Joyful Wisdom*, trans. Thomas Common (Edinburgh: T.N. Foulis, 1910), 213. Language modernized.

81 *"And this is a universal law"*: Friedrich Nietzsche, *Untimely Meditations*, trans. R.J. Hollingdale (Cambridge: Cambridge University Press, 1983), 63.

81 *"All honor to the ascetic ideal"*: Nietzsche, *On the Genealogy of Morals and Ecce Homo* (trans. Kaufmann and Hollingdale), 158.

82 *"I tried reading books"*: Andrew Sullivan, "I Used to Be a Human Being," *New York*, September 19, 2016, https://nymag.com/intelligencer/2016/09/andrew-sullivan-my-distraction-sickness-and-yours.html

82 *"a form of garbage"*: Neil Postman, *Technopoly* (New York: Alfred A. Knopf, 1992), 69–70.

83 *"when it has no place to go"*: Postman, *Technopoly*, 63.

83 *"As autonomous individuals"*: Matthew Crawford, *The World Beyond Your Head* (New York: Farrar, Straus and Giroux, 2015), 6.

83 *"To attend to anything in a sustained way"*: Crawford, *World Beyond Your Head*, 15.

84 *"Everything begins with attention"*: Alan Jacobs, "Attending to Technology: Theses for Disputation," *New Atlantis* 48 (Winter 2016).

85 *As Postman notes*: Postman, *Technopoly*, 75.

87 *"I shall be asked why"*: Friedrich Nietzsche, *Ecce Homo*, trans. R.J. Hollingdale (London: Penguin Books, 1991), 36.

87 *"I am much more interested in a question"*: Friedrich Nietzsche, *Basic Writings of Nietzsche*, trans. Walter Kaufmann (New York: Modern Library, 1992), 693.

87 *"During my Basel period"*: Nietzsche, *Basic Writings* (Kaufmann trans.), 697.

88 *"A strong and well-constituted man"*: Nietzsche, *On the Genealogy of Morals and Ecce Homo* (trans. Kaufmann and Hollingdale), 129.

88 *"I moved out of the house of the scholars"*: Friedrich Nietzsche, *Thus Spoke Zarathustra*, trans. Graham Parkes (Oxford: Oxford University Press, 2005), 108.

88 *Nietzsche was, from his earliest writings*: Nietzsche, *Untimely Meditations* (Hollingdale trans.), 59.

90 *"A book like this, a problem like this"*: Friedrich Nietzsche, *Daybreak*, trans. R.J. Hollingdale (Cambridge: Cambridge University Press, 1982), 5.

90 *"go aside, to take time, to become still"*: Nietzsche, *Daybreak* (Hollingdale trans.), 5.

90 *the opportunity to go slow in an "age of 'work' "*: Friedrich Nietzsche, *The Dawn of Day*, trans. J.M. Kennedy (New York: Macmillan, 1911), 8–9.

91 *"Young people today process more words"*: Mark Bauerlein, "Nietzsche on Slow Reading," *Chronicle of Higher Education*, September 22, 2008, https://www.chronicle.com/blogs/brainstorm/nietzsche-on-slow-reading

92 *"We are in great haste"*: Henry David Thoreau, *The Writings of Henry David Thoreau*, vol. II (Cambridge, MA: Riverside Press, 1906), 57–58.

93 *"The art of not reading is a very important one"*: Arthur Schopenhauer, *Essays and Aphorisms*, trans. R.J. Hollingdale (London: Penguin, 1970), 210.

93 *"What is it, fundamentally"*: Nietzsche, *Basic Writings of Nietzsche* (Kaufmann trans.), 680–81.

94 *"In all that I say, conclude, or think"*: Friedrich Nietzsche, *Human, All Too Human*, trans. Paul Cohn, vol. 2 (New York: Macmillan, 1911), 178.

95 *"One thing is necessary above all"*: Nietzsche, *On the Genealogy of Morals and Ecce Homo* (trans. Kaufmann and Hollingdale), 23.

95 *"I almost always seek refuge"*: Nietzsche, *Basic Writings* (Kaufmann trans.), 699.

95 *"I hate to read new books"*: William Hazlitt, "On Reading Old Books," *Selected Essays* (Cambridge: Cambridge University Press, 1917), 60.

96 *"Once and for all," he writes*: Friedrich Nietzsche, *Twilight of the Idols and The Anti-Christ*, trans. R.J. Hollingdale (London: Penguin Books, 1968), 33.

96 *"What am I really doing"*: Nietzsche, *Dawn of Day* (Kennedy trans.), 197–98.

98   *"Forgetting is essential to action"*: Nietzsche, *Untimely Meditations* (Hollingdale trans.), 62.

99   *"With one quick look"*: Jorge Luis Borges, "Funes, His Memory," *Collected Fictions*, trans. Andrew Hurley (London: Penguin, 1999), 135.

99   *"to think is to ignore (or forget) differences"*: Borges, "Funes, His Memory" (Hurley trans.), 137.

100   *"Some memories are good"*: "The Woman Who Can Remember Everything," *The Telegraph*, May 9, 2008, https://www.telegraph.co.uk/news/newstopics/howaboutthat/1940420/The-woman-who-can-remember-everything.html. More context is provided in a 2019 *Wired* article: Gary Marcus, "Total Recall: The Woman Who Can't Forget," *Wired*, March 23, 2009, https://www.wired.com/2009/03/ff-perfectmemory/.

100   *"Forgetfulness is . . . an active"*: Friedrich Nietzsche, *On the Genealogy of Morals,* trans. Douglas Smith (Oxford: Oxford University Press, 1996), 39.

101   *the scientific worldview "hates forgetting"*: Nietzsche, *Untimely Meditations* (Hollingdale trans.), 120.

103   *"It is always the same thing"*: Nietzsche, *Untimely Meditations* (Hollingdale trans.), 62.

104   *"The event of the day sweeps you along"*: Nietzsche, *Dawn of Day* (Kennedy trans.), 180.

104   *"How can anyone become a thinker"*: Friedrich Nietzsche, *Human, All Too Human*, trans. R.J. Hollingdale (Cambridge: Cambridge University Press, 1986), 390.

104   *"At times when I am deeply sunk in work"*: Nietzsche, *Ecce Homo* (Hollingdale trans.), 26.

105   *"To set to early in the morning"*: Friedrich Nietzsche, *Ecce Homo*, trans. Anthony Ludovici (New York: Macmillan, 1911), 48.

105   *"The scholar who, in truth, does little else"*: Nietzsche, *Ecce Homo* (Ludovici trans.), 48.

105   *"Smartphones are the primary enabler"*: Cal Newport, *Digital Minimalism: Choosing a Focused Life in a Noisy World* (New York: Portfolio/Penguin, 2019), 115.

105 *"Technology gives us more and more"*: Sherry Turkle, *Alone Together* (New York: Basic Books, 2011), 284–85.

106 *"Noise murders thought"*: Friedrich Nietzsche, *Thus Spoke Zarathustra*, trans. Walter Kaufmann (New York: Modern Library, 1995), 226.

106 *"All of you for whom furious labor"*: Nietzsche, *Thus Spoke Zarathustra* (Parkes trans.), 40.

107 *"Why this solitude?"*: Nietzsche, *Dawn of Day* (Kennedy trans.), 341–42.

107 *"Contact with friends and books is good"*: Robert Miner, "Nietzsche on Friendship," *Journal of Nietzsche Studies* 40 (2010): 47–69.

107 *"Take healthy eating as an analogy"*: Tony Fadell, "The iPhone Changed Our Lives. Now Apple Needs to Tackle Addiction," *Wired*, April 14, 2018, https://www.wired.co.uk/article/tony-fadell-apple-iphone-addiction -control-design

108 *"rejecting, sifting, transforming, ordering"*: Nietzsche, *Human, All Too Human* (Hollingdale trans.), 83.

Four: Wisdom Won by Walking

112 *Socrates's problem was that*: Friedrich Nietzsche, *Basic Writings of Nietzsche*, trans. Walter Kaufmann (New York: Modern Library, 1992), 727.

112 *"Socrates was a misunderstanding"*: Friedrich Nietzsche, *The Portable Nietzsche*, trans. Walter Kaufmann (New York: Penguin Books, 1982), 478–79.

112 *"We speak not strictly and philosophically"*: David Hume, *A Treatise of Human Nature* (Oxford: Clarendon Press, 1960), 415.

113 *"It is not contrary to reason to prefer the destruction"*: Hume, *A Treatise*, 416.

113 *"emotions occur in steps"*: Jonathan Haidt, *The Righteous Mind* (New York: Vintage Books, 2013), 52–53.

113 *"I have argued that the Humean model"*: Haidt, *Righteous Mind*, 79.

114 *"Thoughts are the shadows of our feelings"*: Friedrich Nietzsche, *The Joyous Science*, trans. R. Kevin Hill (London: Penguin Books, 2018), 154.

114 *"We think through the body"*: Matthew Crawford, *The World Beyond Your Head* (New York: Farrar, Straus and Giroux, 2015), 51.

115 *"Sit as little as possible"*: Nietzsche, *Basic Writings* (Kaufmann trans.), 695–96.

115 *"Only ideas won by walking have any value"*: Friedrich Nietzsche, *Twilight of the Idols and The Anti-Christ*, trans. R.J. Hollingdale (London: Penguin Books, 1968), 36.

115 *"I think that I cannot preserve my health"*: Quoted in Cal Newport, *Digital Minimalism: Choosing a Focused Life in a Noisy World* (New York: Portfolio/Penguin, 2019), 122.

116 *"Technology proposes itself"*: Sherry Turkle, *Alone Together* (New York: Basic Books, 2011), 1.

117 *"Every hour I spent online was not spent"*: Andrew Sullivan, "I Used to Be a Human Being," *New York*, September 19, 2016, https://nymag.com/intelligencer/2016/09/andrew-sullivan-my-distraction-sickness-and-yours.html

118 *"What a ridiculous state of affairs this is"*: Nathan Jurgenson, "The IRL Fetish," *New Inquiry*, June 28, 2012, https://thenewinquiry.com/the-irl-fetish/

118 *"The logic of social media follows us"*: Jurgenson, "The IRL Fetish."

119 *"We have never appreciated a solitary stroll"*: Jurgenson, "The IRL Fetish."

121 *"Computer interfaces, and the increasingly intelligent software"*: Newport, *Digital Minimalism*, 181.

122 *"the natural world begins to seem bland"*: Crawford, *World Beyond Your Head*, 17.

123 *"To invent fables about a world"*: Nietzsche, *Portable Nietzsche* (Kaufmann trans.), 484.

124 *"Ten years have elapsed"*: Friedrich Nietzsche, *Ecce Homo*, trans. Anthony Ludovici (New York: Macmillan, 1911), 130.

124 *"For my part, these things have never"*: Nietzsche, *Ecce Homo* (Ludovici trans.), 130.

124 *"It's a gift to exist"*: From Stephen Colbert, interview by Anderson Cooper, August 2019, https://twitter.com/AC360/status/1162183695270387712/video/1.

126 Many of our *"chronic illnesses of the soul"*: Friedrich Nietzsche, *The Dawn of Day*, trans. J.M. Kennedy (New York: Macmillan, 1911), 329.

127   *"Habit seems to work from the outside in"*: Crawford, *World Beyond Your Head*, 39.

129   *"Everyone should sometimes write by hand"*: These are three of the theses from Alan Jacobs, "Attending to Technology: Theses for Disputation," *New Atlantis* 48 (Winter 2016).

137   *"Oh, this moderation in 'joy'"*: Friedrich Nietzsche, *The Joyful Wisdom*, trans. Thomas Common (Edinburgh: T.N. Foulis, 1910), 255.

138   *"Dionysus—under the name Zagreus"*: "Dionysus," *Encyclopedia Britannica*, May 26, 2021, https://www.britannica.com/topic/Dionysus.

138   *"the basic understanding of the unity of all things"*: Friedrich Nietzsche, *The Birth of Tragedy*, trans. Shaun Whiteside (London: Penguin Books, 1993), 52.

139   *"This hope alone casts a ray of joy"*: Nietzsche, *Birth of Tragedy* (Whiteside trans.), 52.

139   *"Today I find it an impossible book"*: Nietzsche, *Birth of Tragedy* (Whiteside trans.), 5.

140   *"Today our whole attitude towards nature"*: Friedrich Nietzsche, *On the Genealogy of Morals*, trans. Douglas Smith (Oxford: Oxford University Press, 1996), 92.

140   *"We are unknown to ourselves"*: Friedrich Nietzsche, *On the Genealogy of Morals and Ecce Homo*, trans. Walter Kaufmann and R.J. Hollingdale (New York: Vintage Books, 1967), 15.

Five: The Gay Science?

141   *"What if one day or night a demon came"*: Friedrich Nietzsche, *The Joyous Science*, trans. R. Kevin Hill (London: Penguin Books, 2018), 220–21.

144   *"Where are the new physicians of the soul"*: Friedrich Nietzsche, *Daybreak*, trans. R.J. Hollingdale (Cambridge: Cambridge University Press, 1982), 33.

145   *"The worst disease of mankind"*: Friedrich Nietzsche, *The Dawn of Day*, trans. J.M. Kennedy (New York: Macmillan, 1911), 56.

147   *"as the screws of a machine"*: Nietzsche, *Dawn of Day* (Kennedy trans.), 214–16.

148   *"I know of no other way"*: Friedrich Nietzsche, *Ecce Homo*, trans. R.J. Hollingdale (London: Penguin Books, 1991), 37.

149   *"only believe in a God"*: Friedrich Nietzsche, *Thus Spake Zarathustra*, trans. Thomas Common (Mineola, NY: Dover Publications, 1999), 24.

149   *"All good things laugh"*: Friedrich Nietzsche, *Thus Spoke Zarathustra*, trans. Graham Parkes (Oxford: Oxford University Press, 2005), 257.

149   *"Stendhal is one of the happiest accidents"*: Friedrich Nietzsche, *Ecce Homo*, trans. Anthony Ludovici (New York: Macmillan, 1911), 38–39.

150   He would eat nothing but *"lightly brewed tea"*: Sander Gilman, ed., *Conversations with Nietzsche* (New York: Oxford University Press, 1987), 111.

150   *"we are always finally recompensed"*: Friedrich Nietzsche, *The Joyful Wisdom*, trans. Thomas Common (Edinburgh: T.N. Foulis, 1910), 258–59.

151   *"At an absurdly tender age"*: Nietzsche, *Ecce Homo* (Ludovici trans.), 54.

151   *"the hermit of Sils-Maria"*: Friedrich Nietzsche, *Nietzsche: Unpublished Letters*, ed. Kurt Leidecker (New York: Philosophical Library, 1959), 121.

151   *"Things are different with me"*: Nietzsche, *Nietzsche: Unpublished Letters*, 69.

151   *"Even if I should, by chance"*: Nietzsche, *Nietzsche: Unpublished Letters*, 96.

152   *"So then I really am going"*: Gilman, *Conversations with Nietzsche,* 123.

152   Nietzsche replied with a note: Nietzsche, *Nietzsche: Unpublished Letters*, 107.

152   The place *"does not agree with me"*: Nietzsche, *Nietzsche: Unpublished Letters*, 113.

152   *"Better to die than live* here": Friedrich Nietzsche, *Human, All Too Human*, trans. Marion Faber and Stephen Lehmann (London: Penguin Books, 1994), 6.

153   *"Who today still feels a serious obligation"*: Nietzsche, *Human, All Too Human* (Faber and Lehmann trans.), 29.

153   *"Nietzsche hated the normal person"*: Gilman, *Conversations with Nietzsche*, 145.

153   the friends he lacks: See Friedrich Nietzsche, *Human, All Too Human*, trans. Helen Zimmern, vol. 1 (London: George Allen and Unwin, 1909), aphorism 2 in any translation.

153   *"Technology is seductive"*: Sherry Turkle, *Alone Together* (New York: Basic Books, 2011), 1.

154   But *"when people talk about the pleasures"*: Turkle, *Alone Together*, 13.

154 *"Distinguishing between genuine insights"*: From Richard Schact's intro-
     duction to Friedrich Nietzsche, *Human, All Too Human*, trans. R.J.
     Hollingdale (Cambridge: Cambridge University Press, 1986), xvi.

155 *"Followers I do not want"*: Nietzsche, *Nietzsche: Unpublished Letters*, 77.

156 *"We are faltering"*: Nietzsche, *Human, All Too Human* (Hollingdale
     trans.), 118.

157 *"does not stem from ill will toward technology"*: Albert Borgmann, *Tech-
     nology and the Character of Contemporary Life* (Chicago: University of
     Chicago Press, 1984), 248.

INDEX